Muslim Heritage and the 21st Century

Muhammad Ahsan

Ta-Ha Publishers Ltd.
1 Wynne Road
London SW9 0BB
UK

Copyright © 1422/2002 Ta-Ha Publishing Ltd.

Published by:

Ta-Ha Publishers Ltd.
1 Wynne Road
London SW9 0BB

All rights reserved. No part of this publication may be reproduced, stored in any retrieval system, or transmitted in any form or by any means, electronic or otherwise, without written permission of the publishers.

By: Muhammad Ahsan
General Editor: Afsar Siddiqui
Edited by: Abdassamad Clarke

British Library Cataloguing in Publication Data
Ahsan, Muhammad
Muslim Heritage and the 21st Century
1. Arts, Islamic 2. Islamic countries – Civilisation
I. Title II. Clarke, Abdassamad
700.9'17671

ISBN 1 84200 0330

Typeset by: Bookwright.
Email: bookwright@bogvaerker.dk
Web-site: http://www.bogvaerker.dk/Bookwright
Printed by: Deluxe Printers, London. Tel: 0208-965 1771

Contents

Dedication v
Foreword vi

1. Islamic Approach to Knowledge 1
   1.1 Islam and the Expansion of Knowledge 2
   1.2 Islam and Knowledge in the Light of the Qur'an and Hadith 2
   1.3 Non-Muslims Writers on the Prophet's Teachings 4
   1.4 Non Muslim Scholars on Islam and Scientific Development 5

2. Physical Sciences 9
   2.1 Mathematics 10
   2.2 Astronomy 12
   2.3 Geography and Geology 13
   2.4 Cartography 15
   2.5 Physics 17
   2.6 Mechanics and Optics 18

3. Biological Sciences 19
   3.1 Zoology 20
   3.2 Botany 22
   3.3 Medicine and Surgery 23
   3.4 Chemistry 26

4. Agricultural Sciences 28
   4.1 Agriculture in the Early Islamic Period 29
   4.2 Agricultural Development of Early Muslims 33
   4.3 The Muslim Horticultural System 38
   4.4 Agricultural Research and Publications 44

5. Social Sciences and other Disciplines 48
   5.1 History and Sociology 49
   5.2 Philosophy 50
   5.3 Law and Independent Judiciary 51
   5.4 Literature and Poetry 52
   5.5 Political System and Governance 53
   5.6 Navigation and Shipbuilding 54
   5.7 Architecture 57
   5.8 Painting 58
   5.9 Oratory 59
   5.10 Educational Institutions and Libraries 59
   5.11 Calligraphy 61

6. Review and Reflections 63
   6.1 Factors for the Rise and Fall of Muslims 64
   6.2 State of the Contemporary Muslim World 72
   6.3 The Ummah and the 21st Century 75

Further Reading 85
Basic Data on the Muslim World 93

Dedication

To the young inhabitant of the 'global-village' who knows much about contemporary advances in the West, but is unaware of the advances of Muslims in history.

Foreword

Throughout history, civilisation has continuously passed through stages, and records bear out the progress achieved by humankind in ancient Egypt and Greece. After this, there was the golden age of scientific progress during the heyday of Muslim rule. When Muslims faced decline on account of their internal bickering and other factors, the Europeans took over not only wealth and territory from them, but they established their supremacy in the domain of technical scientific knowledge as well. Little wonder then that a young student today knows that radio, tape recorders and telephones are inventions of the West, yet he (or she) is ignorant of the fact that Muslims were the first to evolve some of our most common mathematical formulae and measure the radius of the earth. Contemporary youth is familiar with the contributions of western scholars to zoology and botany yet he knows nothing about the fact that Muslims had introduced several centuries ago the artificial insemination of animals and grafting of fruit-bearing plants. The discovery of America is attributed to Columbus yet it is unknown to him that Arab navigators had reached the shores of the New World much earlier than Columbus, something borne out by the testimony of historical evidence.

Scholars have made many attempts to remove the widespread ignorance about Muslims' contribution to knowledge. There is no shortage of voluminous works on the subject. However, most of these scholarly works are beyond the reach and understanding of the general public and young students. Realising this need, the present work has been compiled in order to show a glimpse of the rich Muslim heritage. Since this book is primarily designed for people in general and young students in particular, footnotes and references are avoided to maintain adequate comprehension at that level. Suggestions for improving the standard of this work and for broadening its scope and range are welcome.

Muhammad Ahsan
London

1.
Islamic Approach to Knowledge

Allah showed great kindness to the muminun when He sent a Messenger to them from among themselves to recite His Signs to them and purify them and teach them the Book and Wisdom,… (Qur'an 3:164)

1.1 Islam and the Expansion of Knowledge

One of the chief purposes of the Prophet Muhammad's ﷺ advent was to enrich not only the Arabs but also the whole world with knowledge and civilisation. His role as a teacher and educator emerges very clearly in the works on his biography. It is reported on the authority of 'Abdullah ibn 'Amr ibn al-'As that one day when the Prophet ﷺ came to the mosque in Madinah, he noted two groups of the Companions, one was engaged in reciting the Qur'an and making supplications while the other was preoccupied with learning and teaching. He remarked that both the groups were performing something good and said: 'I have been sent as a teacher'. He joined the latter.

1.2 Islam and Knowledge in the Light of the Qur'an and Hadith

The Qur'an repeatedly stresses the importance of knowledge and of reflection. It may be judged best in the light of the fact that in the first verse of the Qur'an which was revealed, Allah asks man to read or recite:

> Recite: In the Name of your Lord who created, created man from clots of blood. (96:1-2)

The same truth is reiterated at other places.

> ...and say:'My Lord, increase me in knowledge.' (20:111).

> Allah will raise in rank those of you who have iman and those who have been given knowledge. (58:11).

On studying the Qur'an one notes that Allah directs humankind to reflect upon natural phenomena such as the creation of the heavens and the earth, seasonal changes, alternation of day and night and the laws of nature governing the seas, clouds, winds, the moon and the sun. The Qur'an asks humankind also to think about the factors responsible for the rise and fall of nations. A human being should study the rising and setting of the sun, the flowing springs, valleys and mountains, orchids of date-palms, vineyards, the bright blue sky and the ships sailing on the seas.

Deutsch, too, places on record his admiration for the teachings of the Qur'an. He says that the Qur'an is the book which enabled the Arabs to appear in European lands as saviours to rekindle the light of knowledge in a world which was steeped in darkness. They revived Hellenic learning and wisdom. They taught the West philosophy, astronomy and medicine. They brought up the nascent sciences. They preceded us on the firmament and have reserved a place for themselves in the front. We should lament the day of the fall of Granada.

Maurice Bucaille, a famous contemporary French physician, states:

> 'For many centuries, man was unable to study them [the encyclopedic knowledges necessary to understand the Qur'an] because he did not possess sufficient means. It is only today that numerous verses of Qur'an dealing with natural phenomenon have become fully comprehensible. I should even go so far as to say that in the twentieth century, with its compartmentalisation of ever-increasing knowledge, it was not always easy for an average scientist to understand everything he reads in the Qur'an on such subjects, without having resource to specialised research. This means that to understand all such verses of the Qur'an one is today required to have an absolutely encyclopedic knowledge, by which I mean, one which embraces very many disciplines.'

Apart from the Qur'an, the Prophet's ﷺ teachings also emphasise the importance of knowledge. In Islam faith and knowledge are inextricably interwoven. Some of the sayings of the Prophet ﷺ on the importance of knowledge are: 'Whoever seeks a way for pursuing knowledge, Allah will facilitate his admission to the Garden' (Muslim). 'One who sets out from his home seeking knowledge pursues the way in the cause of Allah' (Bukhari and

Muslim). 'It is obligatory on every Muslim to seek knowledge' (Ibn Majah). 'The angels spread their wings for a student (Bukhari).

1.3 Non-Muslims Writers on the Prophet's Teachings

Gandhi observed:

> 'On studying the Prophet's life I have grown in my conviction that Islam did not spread by the sword. Rather the real reasons for the success of Islam were the exceptional simplicity and selflessness of the Prophet, respect for men and women, utmost concern for his companions, boldness and fearlessness, unflinching trust in Allah and total confidence in the truthfulness of his mission. These features helped overcome all the obstacles in their sweep.'

Lala Bishan Das comments:

> 'To say a few words about the Prophet Mohammad's glory on my part amounts to temerity. I am too minor to express an opinion about him. For he was the master of all saints and spiritual figures, an illustrious messenger and leader of the leaders of faith. As the sun does not stand in need of a lamp, a mortal human being's praise for him cannot add to his prestige. He was an embodiment of greatness and glory. At the time of his advent the condition of Arabia was horrible. Evil deeds and immorality were rife. The Arabs were opposed tooth and nail to monotheism. Even fathers married their own daughters without any compunction. There were idols everywhere, in homes and in the marketplace. Social evils plagued life. People groaned under the shackles of superstition. Only the Prophet had the courage and resolve to preach monotheism in a society, which was wedded to unbelief. More importantly, he was not a literate person. Yet he planted the sapling of monotheism in the desert of Arabia with firm commitment. Today it has grown into an over-arching tree, with branches in every part of the world. The love, honour and loyalty in which he is remembered is not shared

by any saint, messenger or spiritual figure. The spirit of fraternity characterising Islam is unique in world history. He established Islam on such firm roots that it has not been possible for any one to shake its foundations. All these points go to prove that he was an exceptional person gifted with special power, the messenger of God for the reform of mankind.'

1.4 Non Muslim Scholars on Islam and Scientific Development

Those ignorant of the fundamental principles of Islam are in the forefront of attacking it. One of their allegations is that Islam is opposed to science. However, most scholars think otherwise. Many European scholars have openly acknowledged the great contribution of Muslims to learning. Briffault remarks that there is no single aspect of the progress attained by Europe which does not bear out the impact of Islamic civilisation upon it. Its influence on the opening stages of European civilisation is unmistakable.

In his *History of the Arabs*, Philip Hitti says that in their Spanish period, Muslims left a deep imprint on learning in medieval Europe. It led to a glorious era of knowledge and civilisation. From the eighth to the thirteenth centuries, Arabic speaking scholars were the torchbearers of culture and civilisation in the world. It was they who developed philosophy and other branches of knowledge. They made substantial contributions to every discipline. They promoted knowledge so much so that it led to the Renaissance in Western Europe. Similarly, Lucen Lerec states that the world will not witness again the impressive spectacle presented by Arabic speaking Muslims in the ninth century. They dominated every branch of Greek learning.

Julian Ruskus, a scholar of the University of Berlin maintains that Arabic alchemy greatly improved upon Greek alchemy and influenced Western alchemy so much that students of the medieval period took a very keen interest in its study. They sought to recover what had once led them to great heights. In the issue of *Islamic Review* of March 1955, John W. Campbell writes that Islam obtained all that for which other nations did not try. Islam opened the way for science, a feat which could not be accomplished even by the Romans and Greeks. According to him, one of the main reasons for the ignorance of Europeans about Muslim contributions is that by the time the 'dark ages' ended in Europe, the Romans and Greeks, who had once been the bitter enemies of Christianity, had shed their hostility, and by 1400, Islam was their common enemy. After the revival of knowledge, Europeans turned more to Roman and Greek philosophy rather than paying any tribute to its enemy.

Robert Briffault reinforces Campbell's observation by opining that science owes it existence to Arabic speaking Muslims. Whatever we know as science, developed as a result of the new modes of scientific enquiry and experiment carried out by Europeans. These modes were unknown to the Greeks. However, it was the Muslims who familiarised Europeans with these methods. In his book, Draper supports Campbell's viewpoint in asserting that the Muslim victors once again turned Egypt into a dignified power in the world. Not only did Muslims preserve ancient Greek works, they elaborated and improved upon them. A contribution to *Reader's Digest* (1955) brings to light the scientific method which Islam infused into the human mind. It promotes the rational faculty and scientific method. The author comments that in every respect the Prophet Muhammad ﷺ represented dynamism. When his little son Ibrahim died, there was a solar eclipse. People whispered among themselves that it was a divine expression of grief over his death. Upon hearing this, he ﷺ said that the solar eclipse is a natural phenomenon and that it is sheer absurdity to ascribe it to someone's death or birth.

In a similar vein, S.P. Scott writes that there is no achievement of ancient or recent times which can equal the Muslim contribution. No one ever accomplished so much and so soon as the Muslims did. Nor did anyone leave such an imprint upon the growth of the mind of a human generation as they achieved. During Muslim rule, Andalusia reached heights of glory in only half a century to which Italy could not even come close in its one thousand year long history. In his other book, *Our Elder Brethren*, he records that what Muslims achieved in the domain of knowledge in six centuries is much more than what they gained by the sword.

In the opinion of Gregory, the Muslims had surpassed everyone in their scholarly, technological and industrial attainments. In his book, Victor Robson contrasts Muslim learning with the ignorance in the West. In his view, while Europe was steeped in darkness, Cordoba (Qurtuba) was full of light. Europe was full of filth whereas there were one thousand public baths in Cordoba. Europe abounded in insects and flies while it was a common practice of everyone to change undergarments everyday in Cordoba. Mud filled alleys in Europe while there were pavements in Cordoba. European nobles could not write their names while school children were a common sight in Cordoba.

In *The General History of Europe*, Thatcher pays tribute to Muslim contributions to learning. The author argues that Muslims raised the discipline of mathematics on the Greek foundations. Arab mathematicians invented the 'zero'. Symbols were used for the first time by Muhammad ibn Musa al-Khwarizmi and he classified numbers in natural categories. The Arabs developed trigonometry and made substantial additions to this discipline. In physics, they invented the pendulum and wrote books on optics. They boosted the study of astronomy and set up many observatories. They invented astronomical equipment that is used up to this day. They could work out the angular relationship between the sun and the earth and the dates on which day and night were equal. Their knowledge of astronomy was astounding. In pharmacology they made great advances on the Greek heritage. They studied surgery and public hygiene thoroughly. Their pharmacological works are akin to modern materia-medica. Many of their methods of treatment are in vogue even today. The Muslim surgeons were familiar with anaesthesia. Their contribution to herbal medicine is immense. They achieved all this in an age when the use of medicine in Europe was almost taboo on religious grounds. The only treatment was the performance of certain religious rituals by the clergy. Muslims were the real masters of pharmacology.

The pivotal principle in obtaining knowledge is that the interdisciplinary links between subjects be established. If man's being is divided and placed in different categories, the truth cannot be unravelled. For grasping the truth, spiritual and mental unity is needed. It is not otherwise possible to conceive a comprehensive concept of knowledge. The Islamic viewpoint of science may be summarised thus:

- Islam does not draw any distinction between faith and this world. Rather, both emerge as a unified whole in the Islamic scheme of things.
- This way of life recommends the objective of attaining knowledge as gaining access to the higher reality through spiritual and moral means so that one may reflect upon the material world as a unity and grasp the truth.
- The aim of knowledge is the quest of virtue and condemnation of evil. All the branches of study should converge on this central point, which lends all disciplines a unity.

2.
Physical Sciences

It is an undeniable fact that Muslims made numerous contributions to the physical sciences. By dint of their untiring study and research they enriched the treasuries of knowledge. Abu'l-Husain invented binoculars. The leading Muslim scholar Ibn al-Haytham discovered many truths about the reflection and refraction of light. It is intriguing to note that the same inventions were recorded in Italy three hundred years later. Muslims evolved many formulae of algebra and trigonometry. They measured the solar year. To them belongs also the credit for measuring the circumference of the equator and the radius of the earth. They had unravelled the fact one thousand years ago that the earth revolves around the sun.

2.1 Mathematics

Al-Khwarizmi Muhammad ibn Musa (780-850) is recognised as the father of algebra. His ground-breaking work *Hisab al-Jabr wa'l-Muqabala* was pop popd into Latin by Gerard of Cremona. His work introduced algebra to Europe. Until the sixteenth century, it was the most important mathematical text in European universities. In this work, he presented eight hundred illustrations in point. Al-Khwarizmi developed the discipline of algebra and determined the basic principles of the balancing of two sides of an equation and their geometric interpretation. He also explained the methods of multiplying and dividing algebraic quantities and the addition and subtraction of square roots. One of his important contributions was that he devised a common method of solving second degree equations, which was further refined by Ibrahim al-Farazi at a later date.

Some of the works of another Muslim mathematician, Abu'l-Kamil, are extant. On the basis of these he is hailed as the most eminent mathematician of Islam at the time of the European Middle Ages. His writings on geometry had a lasting influence upon the subject. Abu'l-Kamil made substantial additions to Khwarizmi's *al-Jabr wa'l-Muqabala*. He studied extensively the pentagon and the hexagon, and dealt also with the addition and subtraction of square roots. He was fully conversant with the principles governing equations to the second degree and geometrical concepts. At a later date, Umar al-Khayyam developed further the discipline of algebra. His work, which was republished in 1932 in the USA, promoted the solutions to the algebraic equations to the second degree and triangles. He neatly classified numerous mathematical equations. Abu Bakr Muhammad (d. 1029) also treated several equations. Moreover, he contributed his commentary on Eclidus's work and it was highly popular.

This discussion reflects the fact that the Muslims laid the foundations of algebra and analytical geometry. Many of the fundamental principles which we employ regarding triangles, were prescribed by a non-Muslim scholar, al-Battani (d.930). He worked under Muslim patronage and was the first to talk about the tangent and cotangent. The British scholars Edi Lord (11th century) and De Morley (12th Century) went to Muslim Spain to study mathematics and physics. On their return they popularised the theories of their Muslim teachers. George Perbauch (Professor of Mathematics at Vienna University), wrote a book on his field of specialisation based in the main on Zarqali's writings.

Nasir ad-Din at-Tusi authored several books which deal with rectangular shapes, triangles and spherical shapes. These works enriched the world of scholarship. Kamal ad-Din studied the refraction of sun-rays in rain drops and clarified basic points about the appearance of primary and secondary rainbows. Jabir was looked upon as an authority on algebra in Europe. Likewise, Abu Ishaq Ibrahim and Ali Ibn al-Umrani were accomplished masters in mathematics.

Yusuf al-Mawtan was a member of the Banu Hud tribe. From 1081 to 1085 he was the king of Saragossa. His mathematical work *Istikmal*, is rated by Ibn al-Jahud as equal in worth to the works of Eclidus and al-Majisti. On noting the valuable contributions of Abu'l-Kamil Shuja (d. 955), especially his writings on mathematics, George Sarton opines that his works must be pop popd into English. Abu'l-Wana Buzjani (d. 940) studied the heptagon and laid down the following formulae of trigonometry, which are known to every student.

$Sin (A+B) = Sin A Cos B - Cos A Sin B$
$Sin (A-B) = Sin A Cos B + Cos A Sin B$
$2 Sin^2 A = 1 - Cos A$
$Sin A = 2 Sin Cos A/2$

In addition, the introduction of the cosecant in trigonometry is his other major achievement.

The Arabs passed on much to Europe in the field of mathematics. The very name of the discipline 'algebra' is of Arabic origin. Muslims developed this discipline to great heights. In the thirteenth century, when this Muslim heritage reached Italy, unfortunately, for three centuries no attention was paid in this regard.

2.2 Astronomy

On studying world history it becomes clear that in addition to mathematics, medicine, philosophy and the physical sciences, astronomy was also greatly developed by Muslims. Al-Fazari (706-796), the court astronomer to Caliph Mamun, first pop popd an Indian treatise into Arabic. A team of astronomers led by al-Khwarizmi wrote many treatises on the subject while drawing upon al-Fazari's work. Khalid Abd al-Malik (d. 832) carried out his solar observations in Damascus. He was a leading scholar at Caliph Mamun's court. His son Muhammad and grandson Umar authored *al-Mistah*, an excellent work on the astrolabe. Another court astronomer Abu'l-Abbas compiled his work *Fi Harakaati-s-Samaa'i wa'l-Jawamiy*, which in the twelfth century was pop popd into Latin.

Ibrahim Judhab (d. 776) stands out as an eminent astronomer. He improved considerably on the existing astrolabe. Masha-allah wrote *Kitab al-Ahkaam* on the subject. Jabir ibn Sannan invented the spherical astrolabe, which facilitates the measurement of any angle. 'Abd ar-Rahman as-Sufi of Baghdad (903-986) authored *al-Kawakib ath-Thabitah*. Abu Ma'shar Ja'far Balkhi (d. 886) contributed some works on astrology which won wide acclaim in Europe. In his book *al-Madkhalu fi ilmi'l-Hikmati wa'n-Nujum*, he presented the scientific facts about the tide. Abu Abdullah Muhammad ibn Jabir (d. 929) and Nasir ad-Din at-Tusi compiled work based on their original ideas about the solar eclipse in relation to time, sea level and height.

In his famous work *Rih al-Akbar al-Hakimah*, Musa ibn Yunus (d. 1009) contributed concepts more valuable than those featuring in Ptolemy's works. Later, these contributions of Muslims were pop popd into Latin. Another book compiled by Alphonso X was actually revised versions of ones by Muslims at an earlier date. The same holds true for the writings of Toledo which were based on Zarkali's observations. Copernicus was heavily indebted to Arab astronomers. He pays a glowing tribute to them in his work. In the eleventh century 'Umar Khayyam offered his measurement of the solar year. There is a difference of 1103 seconds between his reckoning and that of present times. In the calendar drawn by him, there is a margin of error of one day in 2770 years while the same margin is one day in 3330 years in the present calendar. Nasir ad-Din at-Tusi helped trigonometry to emerge as a new discipline, independent of astronomy. His work on the movements of stars, introduced by Abu Abdullah al-Batini, was rendered into Latin by Plato of Trivoli.

Apart from the above-mentioned scholars, many others made contributions to astronomy. At the International Astronomical Union conference in 1935, the contribution of Muslim astronomers was openly acknowledged. Phillip Hitti observes in his *History of the Arabs* that Muslim masters have left their indelible imprint. If anyone looks at the names of the stars, he will readily recognise this. Many of their names were borrowed by Europeans from Arabic speaking Muslims. John W. Draper also pays tribute to the Muslim contribution to this subject. In his opinion, it is evident for any student of astronomy that Arabic speakers have left their fingerprints on the stars, as most of their names are Arabic. In fact Muslims received their inspiration from the Qur'an, which declares that for those who are endowed with reason and understanding, there are signs in the creation of the earth, the alternation of day and night, and in the stars and the sky.

2.3 Geography and Geology

Muslim scientists played a key role in expanding and developing the discipline of geography. What accounts in part for this was their fervent desire to perform the duty of *Hajj*. Muslims undertook long journeys to perform *Hajj*. Phillip K. Hitti observes that Muslims had a religious motivation in studying geography especially in view of their duty of doing *Hajj*, in using mosques as educational institutions and in determining the direction of the Ka'bah for offering prayers.

In 870 CE, Abu Zayd travelled to East Asia and chronicled its geographical conditions. His work is the most important source on the subject, predating Marco Polo's voyage to China. In the ninth century, a study was undertaken at the behest of Caliph Mamun to ascertain the density of the earth. Al-Khwarizmi wrote his *Surat al-Ard* in pursuance of the same objective. At the Caliph's directive, he along with his colleagues compiled the map of the world and celestial spheres. They conducted the measurement of a degree of *Khett-i-Nisf an-Nahar* and for them its length was 56.5 miles, only 959 yards more than its reckoning today. The accuracy of their measurement is indeed amazing. According to this reckoning, the diameter and radius of the earth are 20,000 and 6500 miles, respectively. These studies were carried out in the Muslim world at a time when the general belief in Europe was that the earth was flat.

Al-Maqdisi compiled an extensive geographical compendium after his twenty years' long voyages in the middle of the ninth century. In the same period 'Atarid ibn al-Hasib wrote voluminous works on rocks. This valuable work contained a sound discussion on different precious stones. In addition, *Kitab al-Buldan* (891) is another outstanding work, rich in geographical and economic data of that age. Many other works also appeared on the historical and political geography of the Muslim world, the postal system, climate and mineral geography.

Ibn Fadlan (d. 921) travelled north to Russia and authored the first authentic work on the northern pole of the earth. Abu'l-Hasan (d. 957) visited several countries and wrote many works, including his masterpiece *Muruj adh-Dhahab wa Ma'ayin al-Jawahir*. Contained in his works are reliable data on different countries. Other topics treated by him are scientific phenomena, earthquakes, properties of the water in Palestine and geological concepts and issues. He was the first to record an account of the windmills in Sijistan.

In 937, al-Biruni brought into relief certain facts about India adding that it was at one time submerged under water. He also showed that the earth revolves round the sun. He devised a means for extracting minerals. While staying at Nandana castle, about 100 km away from Pakistan's capital, Islamabad, he calculated that the half-radius of the earth is equal to 6339 km. According to the present study it comes to 6354 km, a difference of only 15 km. He also measured the circumference of the earth as 39,869 km, which today is reckoned as 39,996 km. His figure is off the mark by only 127 km. It is well to note that the earth is not exactly spherical and that there is considerable difference in both its radius and circumference.

Abu Zayd al-Balkhi (d. 934) composed a geographical treatise that contained a unique map of the world. It distinctly shows continents, the Gulf of Suez, and seas. In the middle of the ninth century al-Astakhri spelt out the geography of the then Muslim world. In the eleventh century Zarkali made important contributions. In 985, Muhammad al-Maqdisi visited the entire Muslim world and recorded his observations in his compendium. In 1164, Ibn al-Hawaqil produced a work on geography which showed the earth as oval in shape. In 1128, Abu Abdullah Yaqut compiled an extensive geographical dictionary in alphabetical order. Moreover, he authored his *Mu'jam al-Buldan* in six volumes, containing important geographical, physical, historical details and eminent personalities of many towns.

2.4 Cartography

Islamic contributions to cartography were much applauded in European universities. Al-Khwarizmi and Abdullah al-Hamudi are familiar figures in the world of knowledge. However, Abdullah ibn Ahmad is a lesser known name. In his book, *Ahsan at-Taqasim fi Ma'arif al-Aqalim*, he drew many impressive maps of the earth, pointing to deserts, oceans and mountains which appear in golden, bluish and greyish colours respectively. Abu Zayd Ahmad Salih al-Balkhi holds the distinction for producing the earliest atlas, containing the description of the Indian ocean, Morocco, Algeria, Syria, Egypt and the Mediterranean sea. In 934, it was regarded as the official map of the Muslim world. Europeans are familiar with Abdullah al-Idrisi as the most distinguished Muslim geographer. He studied geography for years in Cordoba. His work *Nuzhat al-Mashariq* and *Iftiraq al-Afaq* contained many maps for the benefit of those interested in undertaking voyages.

Columbus was much indebted to Muslim geographers. A South African scholar has argued that Arabs had discovered America centuries before Columbus set out from Spain. His work was published in 1952 and in it he stated that a leading South African anthropologist insisted that it was Muslims, not Christopher Columbus, who discovered America. According to Dr. Jeffrey, a senior lecturer in Social Anthropology, the Muslims predated Columbus in discovering America by five centuries. This scholar found a skull of a Negro in the Rio Grand River and his claim was based on this evidence. For him, the Muslims dominated the Mediterranean Sea by 1000 CE. They had settled on the western coast of Africa and also in America. Columbus had noted small settlements of Africans on the islands. According to him, these were settlements of African slaves belonging to Muslims. This viewpoint is reinforced by the discovery of the skulls of Africans in the Bahamas and by the crops raised in the Caribbean islands. It is likely that many will not subscribe to Dr. Jeffrey's theory. However, another scholar, J.H. Kremer, observed that Muslims might lay their claim to this discovery. There is no denying the fact that, compared to others, the Muslims possessed greater knowledge of the geography of the then known world.

Another interesting point is that about a thousand years ago, the Caliph Harun ar-Rashid intended to build a Suez canal. He constituted a team of seventy scientists that prepared the first map of the earth in 830 CE. In addition to discovering new places and their contribution to geography, Muslim scholars accomplished more important work in determining longitudes and latitudes and in discussing whether the earth is round or flat.

2.5 Physics

Ibn al-Haytham of Cairo (d.1039) was not only an eminent Muslim physicist, he was also a great expert on optics. Chroniclers state that he authored around two hundred books, most of which were on physics. He refuted the then prevalent view that we see things because light emanates from our eyes. Rather, he disclosed the fact that when light strikes on some object, its reflection reaches our eye and we are able to visualise it. He carried out many experiments on reflection and refraction. He was fully confident of the facts about the atmosphere and pointed out that the weight of a body varies in the atmosphere. Some of his experiments were repeated three centuries later in Italy. His treatise on optics promoted this subject in the West. It was used as a source book in the medieval period. Leonardo da Vinci, Bacon and Kepler were influenced by it. Ibn al-Haytham was the one who laid the foundations of the device which today we know as the camera.

Ibn Sina studied at length such natural phenomena as motion, union, energy, space, light and heat. His work *Tas'ah Wasa'il fi'l-Hikmah wa't-Tabi'ah* contained a detailed discussion on weight and gravity. He wrote ten books on physics. Umar Khayyam discovered ways for ascertaining the impurity of metals. Abu'l-Fath al-Khwarizmi, an outstanding Muslim physicist, composed *Kitab al-Mizan wa'l-Hikmah*, which describes the effect of the gravitational force on solid and liquid substances. Moreover, he inferred laws of gravitation and unravelled the fact that the earth draws every thing to its centre.

In addition to the above developments, Abu'l-Husain produced binoculars while the famous Egyptian scientist Ibn Yunus explained the motion of the pendulum. Al-Biruni discussed at length precious stones and the functioning of springs. In his book on the history of photography, Helmet states that the Muslim scholar Ibn al-Haytham was aware of the craft of photography even before 1038 CE.

2.6 Mechanics and Optics

It emerges from the study of history that Muslims surpassed all other communities in their mastery of mechanics and optics. In his article entitled *Muslim Mechanics and Mechanical Devices*, H.J. Winter pays tribute to Muslims. In his opinion, the Arabs and Persians were great experts in producing clocks and various other mechanical devices. The Muslim study of mechanics is not part of Greek thought and heritage. They made noteworthy additions to the subject, thanks to their ingenuity.

Fakhr ad-Din Ridwan al-Khurasani is known also as *Ibn as-Sa'ati* (son of the clock) as a mark of honour for his command of his subject, for he was an accomplished master in the manufacture of clocks. At the behest of Malik al-'Adil, in 1174, he produced the clock which was installed at the gate of Jami'ah Damascus.

After 900 CE, there were many advances in both theoretical and applied mechanics that greatly improved the functioning of wheels, pistons, bearings, and windmills. The significant work *Kitab al-Mizan wa'l-Hikmah* was written during this period and dealt with mechanical equipment related to oars and wheels etc. Al-Huzeni contributed a book on balance. Earlier, Umar Khayyam and al-Muzaffar ibn Isma'il al-Asfarin had contributed much to this discipline.

More evidence of Islamic impact on mathematics in Europe is given by the fact that Arabic expressions such as algebra and algorithm were incorporated into Latin. The eighth century scholar, Qadi Abu Bakr employed mathematical concepts, especially a kind of relativity theory in dealing with time and space.

3.
Biological Sciences

The Muslims were so advanced in pharmacology that they did not let anyone die before his natural death. For eight centuries, they not only maintained supremacy in the medical world but many Muslim medical authorities also served as teachers in European universities. Muslims held the distinction of producing sulphuric acid. They were the pioneers in the artificial insemination of animals. There were centres of higher education and research in all major towns, which contributed to scientific progress.

3.1 Zoology

With reference to the context, here at first, it would be appropriate to review the Islamic approach to the welfare of animals. A hadith is cited in Bukhari, Muslim, Malik and Abu Dawud that once a man felt thirsty on his journey. He found a well on the roadside and took water from it. Later, he saw a dog panting with thirst and looking for water. On observing the dog, that person was reminded of his own thirst. He returned to the well, filled his leather sock with water and offered it to the dog. Allah appreciated his kindness and pardoned his wrong actions. On hearing this, a companion asked the Prophet ﷺ whether one would be rewarded by Allah for kindness towards animals. To this the Prophet ﷺ replied in the affirmative, asserting that one will earn a reward for being kind to every living being, including animals.

Islam prohibits any animal being denied food or water. Once, the Prophet ﷺ passed by a camel who appeared emaciated owing to hunger. He directed that one should fear Allah regarding animals, for they cannot express themselves. Islam forbids gaming (i.e., bull and cock fighting) or even hunting as mere sport. The Prophet ﷺ is on record as saying that whoever kills even a bird for fun will have a complaint against him on the Day of Judgment. That bird will complain that he had been killed only for entertainment, not for any benefit. The Prophet also forbade that any animal be branded with fire. Abu Dawud relates it on Jabir's authority that once a donkey passed near the Prophet ﷺ, which was branded on the face. On noting this the Prophet ﷺ said: 'Cursed be him who branded it.'

As it is a wrong actions to hurt or torment animals, doing good to them brings one divine reward. Ibn Majah reports that once a companion told the Prophet ﷺ that he had built tanks for storing drinking water for his camels. At times stray camels drank water from it. He asked whether he would earn any reward for offering water to other camels. To this he ﷺ replied that one would be rewarded for showing a favour to any thirsty animal.

Kindness towards animals is an illustrious aspect of Islamic civilisation. During the glorious period of Islam, the Caliphs issued directives to people, forbidding them to cause any hurt to animals. Rather, they were asked to be kind towards them. Once Caliph 'Umar ibn al-Khattab saw someone pulling a goat by its leg in order to slaughter it. He reproached that person and directed him to take it kindly to the site of its slaughter. Another Caliph, 'Umar ibn 'Abd al-'Aziz, also issued directives to his governors to ensure that people did not hurt or lash their horses. He directed Muslims on patrol in the society that they should not let people burden horses with heavy reins. Nor should they allow anyone to use a horsewhip with iron on its end. It was not only people in government, but many voluntary social organisations also worked for the welfare and safety of animals. Such *Awqaf* (plural of *waqf*) are on record as being earmarked for the treatment of sick animals. Some *Waqf* property was reserved as pasture land for old, disabled animals. One of these fields was Marj Akhzar in Damascus which is now used as a playing field by the municipality. Fields were reserved for such old horses which had been discarded by their owners. They were allowed loose in this field to roam freely. All these features point to the spirit of faith expressed as mercy and decency towards animals. This was the environment which encouraged zoologists and scholars to conduct their developmental activities in the fields of animal sciences. Thus that age gave birth to many writers and researchers who devoted their lives to the study of the animal kingdom.

Among medieval Muslim zoologists, al-Jahiz stands out. In his book *al-Hayawan* he discusses extensively a theory of evolution, animal psychology and bacteria. His work contains a wealth of information culled from Greek, Arabic and Persian sources. Some 350 animals were discussed in this book. Al-Jahiz was familiar with Aristotle's views and in his book he criticises him a lot. Another Muslim scholar, Kamal ad-Din ad-Damiri (d. 1405), produced first-rate work on the subject in *Hayat al-Hayawan al-Kubra*. This 1500 pages long book was reprinted several times. One of its hallmarks was that it presented a systematic survey of all the earlier work done in the field of zoology. It was another work, besides al-Jahiz's, which was pop popd into Persian and Turkish.

'Abd al-Malik al-Asma'i (d. 831) was a great scholar and zoologist. His first work was *Kitab al-Khayl* on the horse, the second *Kitab ad-Dakhayel* on the camel, the third on sheep, the fourth *Kitab al-Wuhush* on wild animals and beasts and the last on human-beings, which brought out in an impressive fashion the composition and working of human body parts. Al-Qazwini's work, too, is focused on animals. He categorizes animals in terms of their defence systems and their features.

The famous Muslim scholar Ibn Sina devoted a major part of his book *al-Qanun* to animal sciences. The eighth chapter of it was focused on natural philosophy and physiology. He also conducted a lot of research on the use of animal products as medicine. In the same vein, major portions of the following works abound in useful information about animals such as al-Jilda's *Darrat al-Ghawwas*, Ahmad ibn Yahya al-'Amri's *Masalik al-Absar*, 'Ala' ad-Din al-Jazuli's *Mutali'at-ad-Duar* and Qalqashindi's *Subh al-A'sha*.

3.2 Botany

Muslim botanists vastly enriched this branch of knowledge as a result of their keen interest. The eminent scientist Jabir ibn Hayyan's books *Kitab al-Hudud*, *'Ilm an-Nabat* and *'Ilm al-Filah* cover many issues related to botany. Not only did Muslims study botany in a highly scientific way, but they also examined the spiritual importance of plant life in the universe. Among the notable names in the field of botany who contributed many books on the subject are Abu Nadr ibn Shima'il, Abu Zayd Ansari, Ibn

Sakta' of Kufa, and Abu Sa'id al-Asma'i, author of *an-Nabat wa'sh-Shajar*. In Abu Hanifah ad-Dinawari's *Kitab an-Nabat*, the author brought out the features of many plants within historical and philosophical perspectives. For centuries this work served as a source of information and reference.

In the tenth century, the main focus was on conducting studies of plants in a philosophical vein. Ikhwan as-Safa dealt at length with the physiology, birth and growth of plants and their classification. In Ibn Sina's *at-Tabi'ah* and *ash-Shifa*, there were lengthy discussions on plants. Spanish philosophers of the Muslim period had a keen interest in plants. Ibn Bajah wrote two significant works. The first, *Kitab al-Tajrubatayan* was on the medicinal properties of many herbs and the other one *Kitab fi'n-Nabat* was on the philosophy of plants. Ibn al-Baytar holds the pride of place among botanists. He visited several African countries as part of his academic pursuits and carried out botanical studies. Although both also Ibn al-Baytar and al-Ghafiqi have left works on other disciplines, they reorganised the work on botany by Muslims. Their work won wide acclaim for its high quality.

It needs to be re-emphasised that Muslim botanists dealt with plant taxonomy, physiology, birth, growth and plants' geographical, medical and physical properties. They tried to bring out spiritual and moral lessons. According to Mulla Sadra and some other religious scholars, plants will have an important place in the Garden. In both Persia and Spain, gardens, orchids, trees and flowers assumed great significance during Muslim rule, which is also reflected in Arabic and Persian literature. Muslims' interest in the plants of the Garden led to the emergence of the discipline of botany. For centuries this branch of learning flourished in the Muslim world.

3.3 Medicine and Surgery

Medicine and surgery occupied an important position in the Islamic scheme of things. Both men and women excelled in this subject. During the Prophet's life ﷺ, Umaymah bint Qays al-Ghafarah appeared before the Prophet ﷺ along with her team on the eve of the battle of Khaybar and sought his permission ﷺ to accompany the Muslim army in order to provide the army with their nursing skills. Appreciating her spirit and skill, the Prophet ﷺ granted her permission and she duly performed her duties. It is reported on the authority of Rabi'ah bint Mas'ud that women accompanied the Muslim army and carried out nursing duties and offered them water. There is also on record an account of women who practised medicine. Zaynab of the Bani 'Aud tribe was a famous ophthalmologist. Umm al-Hasan bint Qadi Abi Ja'far was an accomplished scholar having mastery in many subjects. However, she was more famous as a physician. Similarly, the sister and daughters of al-Hafidh Ibn Zubayr, who flourished during the reign of al-Mansur ibn Abi 'Amir, enjoyed fame as physicians. They treated members of the royal family for their gynaecological ailments.

In his *Story of Civilization*, Durrant observes that the Arabs had developed pharmacology so much that they did not let anyone die before his natural death. They not only maintained supremacy in the medical world for eight hundred years but many Arab medical authorities also served as teachers in European universities. Phillip Hitti notes that Arabs carried out extensive studies on the use of medicines and made rapid advances. They were the first to open a drug dispensary and the first institution of pharmacology. They were also the first to compile a pharmacopoeia. Similarly, Gibbon states that more than eight hundred students qualified in pharmacology and secured their licences to practice medicine in Baghdad.

Among Muslim physicians, Ibn Sina was the towering figure. In his magnum opus *al-Qanun fi't-Tibb*, he dealt at length with human body parts, diseases and their symptoms and cure. As to the academic worth of this work, it may be measured against the fact that even today it is valued as an important work. Ibn Sina's works relegated the writings of Galen and others to a secondary position. Many of his books were used as textbooks in European universities.

For three full centuries, *al-Qanun* served as a textbook. Hitti acknowledges that during the twelfth and thirteenth centuries, this work stood out as a guide for medical studies in the West. William Oster remarks that Ibn Sina's *al-Qanun* was studied as the medical bible for so long that it is without any precedent in history. In addition to *al-Qanun*, Ibn Sina authored also *ash-Shifa* which stood out as an invaluable gift of science to the world. He wrote also *al-Adwiya al-Mufrida*, which was reissued as a commemorative volume on his 900th birthday. Although Ibn Sina took medicine to great heights, the golden age of medicine was ushered in by the days of ar-Razi (d. 923). He was an eminent philosopher and physician. In his writings he appeared as a greater medical authority than Galen. Edward G. Browne says of him that of all the Muslim physicians he was the greatest. He was the most extensive writer. Ar-Razi authored more than one hundred books, of which half were on medicine. His twenty-volume long *al-Hawi* was the textbook at Paris University. His other ten volume long *al-Mansuri* was pop popd into several European languages.

Ali Ibn Raben (b. 775, Persia) compiled the first Arabic encyclopedia entitled *Firdaws al-Hikmah*. The manuscript of his work *Hifdh as-Sihhah* adorns to this day the Oxford University library. In his *Zad al-Musafir*, Ahmad Jarrar (d. 900) discusses epidemic diseases – small pox, measles, cold and plague, their causes, precautionary measures and remedy. There was a time when Europe was steeped in darkness whereas the Muslim world recorded amazing advances in pharmacology and medical sciences in general. Muslim physicians were fully conversant with many plants with medical properties. They added numerous plants to the list of medicinal herbs.

According to a French historian, Muslim physicians were aware of more than one hundred ailments of the eye. Abu Musa (777-886) wrote the first treatise on the human eye. Another physician, Abu Ma'shar Ja'far ibn Muhammad (786-886) provided highly useful details about the of growth of the baby in the womb and its delivery in his *Kitab al-Mawlud ar-Rijal wa'n-Nisa'*. It was later pop popd into Latin. Ibn al-Baytar of Damascus (d. 1248) enjoyed a reputation as an outstanding botanist. He classified 1400 plants with medicinal properties. His *al-Adwiya al-Mufridah* stood out as a masterpiece. He compiled this work for the benefit of physicians. Sir Thomas Clifford says that for centuries his work was regarded as the standard on pharmacology in Europe. It discussed surgical equipment extensively. Harvey, a British physician, is credited with the discovery of blood circulation in the body. However, it was Ibn an-Nafis (d. 1288) who was the first to draw attention to it. Harvey borrowed this discovery from him, without acknowledging it and took the credit for himself.

In his encyclopedic work, *Al-Kulliyat fi't-Tibb*, Ibn Rushd disclosed the truth for the first time that after becoming infected once with small pox, one becomes immune to it for ever. He thus laid down the foundation of the study of the immune system. The Arabs hold the distinction of setting up the first pharmacological institutes, mobile clinics and general hospitals. Sir Thomas Clifford notes in *The Encyclopedia Britannica* that many medical terms in vogue in Europe are derived from Arabic such as Rab (Arabic: *Rabb*), Chaleb (Arabic: *Jullab*), Syrup (Arabic: *Sharab*) and Alcohol (Arabic: *al-Kuhul*) etc. Y.C. Young remarks in his *Muslim World*, that Muslims vastly enriched the study of optics and ophthalmology.

3.4 Chemistry

Leading historian Gibbon states that the Muslims had the distinction of introducing and improving the study of chemistry (alchemy or *al-Kimi*). They were the first to draw the distinction between alkali and acid, and to ascertain their interrelationship. They brought into relief the medicinal aspects of poisons and used these in treatment. Jabir bin Hayyan (8th century master) was the first outstanding Muslim chemist. He presented clear and simple principles about chemical studies. He also produced various new compounds. To him, goes the credit for preparing sulphuric acid which is now manufactured in vast quantities for industrial purposes. He discovered also a method for extracting minerals from raw material. He placed great emphasis on the skilful use of alchemy. Among his valuable contributions were his devising ways for manufacturing steel, textile and leather colouring, making waterproof cloth with the help of varnish, protecting iron against rust, making coloured glass with the help of manganese dioxide, and preparing acetic acid. He holds also the distinction of having produced royal-water which dissolves even gold.

Jabir was familiar with numerous chemical reactions, including fractional distillation. His works were widely acclaimed. He improved upon the traditional Aristotelian concept of matter, which was restricted to only the four elements fire, water, air and earth. The sixteenth century European chemists were so influenced by his views that Thomas Martin, the distinguished chemist of Bristol, said that he would be pleased to serve as Jabir's butler. After Jabir, the other most prominent Muslim Chemist was Muhammad Zakariyya ar-Razi (825-925) from Ray (Iran). In his well-equipped personal laboratory, he classified chemical compounds into the following four categories: i) Mineral compounds, ii) Plant compounds, iii) Animal compounds, and, iv) Derived compounds. On deeper reflection, it emerges that the above classification is still valid.

Ibn Sina was regarded as the Aristotle of the Muslim world. He was an expert in chemistry as well. He was the first scientist to refute the popular belief that ordinary metals could be transmuted into gold. This discussion shows that Muslim chemists maintained supremacy in the academic world for a long time. Many treatises of ar-Razi and Ibn Sina on chemistry were used for centuries as textbooks in European universities.

4.
Agricultural Sciences

Agriculture is in fact a branch of biological science, and it was to be discussed within the previous section. The reasons for discussing it in an independent section, are that: i) although with regard to the development of medieval Muslims, enough material is available about other branches of science, agriculture is the only branch that is mostly neglected by historians, ii) in the Islamic philosophy, special emphasis is laid on its importance and development, which at the same time is a science as well as an art, and, iii) Muslims were pioneers in agricultural technologies and they wrote treaties on artificial insemination of animals and plant grafting.

4.1 Agriculture in the Early Islamic Period

In Islamic philosophy, agriculture had its beginning with the creation of the Prophet Adam, peace be upon him, the first man on earth. After his arrival on earth, he naturally stood in need of food. Accordingly, he started farming, in line with the Divine command and acting on his own understanding. When he needed pots for storing food, his wife Hawwa adapted stones for this purpose. Their conduct was scientific. Hawwa may be taken as the first woman scientist and Adam as the first farmer who took up agriculture. According to a report, Adam, peace be upon him, said that the best soil is the blackish one (i.e., rich with organic matter) with a capacity for absorbing water in such a way that it does not become a swamp. Since this soil is marked with the best properties, it is ideally suited for agricultural purposes. Shith, Adam's son also engaged in farming. After the Flood when people came out of the ark, the prophet Nuh, peace be upon him, instructed his followers in the skill of farming. Thus with the passage of time, agriculture developed and new changes marked human life. These advances helped humankind to reach new heights in culture and civilisation. Being central to life, agriculture is extensively covered in both the Qur'an and the Prophet Muhammad's teachings ﷺ. It emerges from the Qur'anic account that the human being had his beginning in an agricultural environment and the first skill he learnt was farming.

Islam had its beginning in a society in which neither agriculture nor industry enjoyed much importance. The main reason for this was that there was little land in Arabia fit for farming. Unlike Persia and Rome, there was no land lordship in Arabia. Thus grain for food was imported from Syria, as there was almost no agricultural activity in southern and central Arabia. Before the Prophet's birth, Makkah had been a major trade centre. Trade delegates from Rome and Persia visited Makkah and had their dealings with local businessmen. The tribe of Quraysh occupied a pivotal position in Makkan trade. There was no central authority or government in Arabia before the Prophet's appearance ﷺ. Nor was there any organised system of tax collection and distribution. However, as the Islamic community was established and expanded, its administration was tuned. Agriculture received a great deal of attention.

On reading Islamic history one notes that the Prophet ﷺ himself instructed his Companions in agriculture. When it was the sowing season, they rallied round him and exchanged their opinions on agricultural practices. Thus they benefited from the experience of one another. It is related on Jabir's authority that the Prophet ﷺ said, 'If a Muslim plants a tree or does farming, he will be rewarded for this act, whether someone eats of it or steals it, be it an animal or bird. The planter will be rewarded, in any case' (*Sahih Bukhari* and *Muslim*). It is evident from his teachings that the Prophet ﷺ encouraged tree planting and farming. In other ahadith (teachings of the Prophet ﷺ), agriculture is cited as an illustration in order to instruct Muslims in knowledge and skill. In view of the importance and usefulness of agriculture in human life the Prophet ﷺ directed the Companions to make the following supplication for increase in agricultural yield, 'O Lord! grant increase in our fruits, in our habitation and in our measuring units.' (*Sahih Bukhari*).

In addition to spiritual teaching and training, the Prophet Muhammad ﷺ as the Messenger of Allah presented a remarkable agricultural model for development. Madinah, the first Islamic community founded by him, was an agricultural community. Agriculture was developed so much in his ten years' rule that the Islamic community did not have to import food grain. Instead, on more than one occasion, surplus grain was exported. The reason for this success was based on his organisational skill, agricultural education, land consolidation, forming cooperative societies, self-help and improvement in irrigational system. Due to the limited scope of this section, only the Muhammadan irrigational system is briefly discussed in the following paragraphs.

4. AGRICULTURAL SCIENCES •• 31

It must be clarified that the Prophet's statements ﷺ were not mere directives. He ﷺ paid full attention to the practical aspects of agriculture. His wisdom ﷺ led to the setting up of an excellent irrigation system for which no precedent is to be found in the history of that region. Under the self-help scheme he ﷺ encouraged people to build a network of small dams. This advanced irrigation method greatly helped the cause of agriculture. The dams built in his days ﷺ were of four types - well dams, spring dams, rainfall dams and mountainous river dams. Well dams were erected facing such wells which lay in disuse during harvest periods. The local administrations (established by him ﷺ) built many such dams. This arrangement made these wells operational throughout the year, with water in reserve. The local administrations were responsible for the maintenance of these dams.

In pre-Islamic days, certain persons had a monopoly over springs. They used them (spring dams) during the sowing season. Their water was, however, wasted and dumped into the desert sands during other times. People did not draw fully on this Divine bounty. The Prophet ﷺ placed these springs in the charge of his administrators. Accordingly, they erected new dams and improved the existing ones. The water thus stored was used throughout the year for irrigation. The other type of dams were rainfall dams and the provincial governments were responsible for their construction and operation. This device helped to regulate water. On the one hand, it protected people against floods and on the other, enough water was stored for irrigating fields. Another type of dam was the mountain river dam. Although, there were only a few mountainous rivers in Arabia, their water was wasted. The Prophet ﷺ directed that dams be built for storing their water. Therefore, in accordance with the Prophetic instructions several new dams were built. The dam on the Ta'if river was very famous. It is noteworthy that these dams were built on the basis of self-help and cooperative work. Even government officials in the Prophet's day ﷺ were volunteers.

During the period of the Rightly Guided Caliphs (i.e., Abu Bakr, 'Umar, 'Uthman and 'Ali, may Allah be pleased with them) the organisation and distribution of agricultural land was in line with the teachings of the Qur'an and the Sunnah. Laws were enacted for ensuring the welfare of farmers. The rulers made sure that if a farmer was disabled or afflicted with some calamity that destroyed his crop or if he was in financial crisis, help was offered to him out of the public treasury. Allowances were paid to disabled farmers. It was in line with the Caliph 'Umar's proclamation, may Allah be pleased with him, that everyone had a right to receive help from the public treasury. In addition, when farmers faced financial difficulty in reclaiming barren land, the administration offered them every help and sanctioned them loans. During Caliph 'Umar's reign, may Allah be pleased with him, particular attention was paid to reclaiming barren land. His tenure was characterised by progress, peace, prosperity, justice and equality. He had issued a general proclamation in accordance with the well known hadith that whoever reclaims barren land will be its owner. As a result of this, barren land was swiftly reclaimed and a higher yield was recorded. Notwithstanding the crisis in Caliph 'Ali's days, may Allah be pleased with him, he also focused his attention on forest development.

Many people are aware of the commands of the Qur'an and ahadith on drinking and irrigation water. However, 'Umar's reforms, may Allah be pleased with him, in this department are relatively less known. During his time water was freely available to everyone and it was not permissible for anyone to prevent someone for taking water. Several canals were constructed during his period. One of them was the Abu Musa Canal in Basra. Once, the people of Basra called on the Caliph 'Umar, may Allah be pleased with him. He enquired from them about local conditions. They complained that they had to carry water for six miles. Immediately, Umar ordered the governor of Basra, Abu Musa al-Ash'ari to have a canal constructed for the local people. As this canal was connected to the Tigris river, everyone was provided with a constant water supply.

Another huge canal was Amir al-Muminin Canal, which was also constructed at Caliph 'Umar's command, may Allah be pleased with him, and which connected the Nile river with the Red Sea. When famine struck the whole of Arabia in 18 AH, he directed all governors to send plenty of grain to Madinah. Although his command was readily followed, the supplies sent from Syria and Egypt by land route took much time to reach Madinah. After careful consideration, he wrote to 'Amr ibn al-'As, the then governor of Egypt, that if the Nile river were connected to the Red Sea, it would minimise the risk of famine in Arabia. Accordingly 'Umar had the canal constructed from Fustat (a town twelve miles from present-day Cairo), to the Red Sea. As a result of this, ships reached the port of Jiddah. Surprisingly, this 69 miles long canal was completed in only six months, and even in the first year of its operation, giant ships used it to reach Jiddah. It is noteworthy, that 'Umar set up a new department, whose assignment was to construct canals in all parts of the country. In Egypt alone, a 120,000 strong labour force was constantly engaged in this business. This was the reason that his efforts brought a green revolution during that time.

4.2 Agricultural Development of Early Muslims

As is obvious from the above, prompted by the Qur'an and Sunnah, Muslims with zeal contributed much to agriculture. They introduced the cultivation of numerous plants such as coffee, oranges, sugar-cane, water melons and apricots etc. to many parts of the Muslim world. They even popularised these in Europe, America and other parts of the world. This helped promote agriculture globally. Muslims were not only scholars, they accomplished much practically in the field. In the following pages, a brief description is made with regard to early agricultural development of Muslims in the different parts of the world.

Andalusia: Since Andalusia (Islamic Spain) was a fertile place, Muslims developed agriculture there along with other disciplines. By dint of their hard work they transformed the whole country into a lush green place and as a result corn and fruit production increased incredibly resulting in economic development. With the passage of time, Muslims even started farming the hills. Muslims in Andalusia excelled in manufacturing fertilisers which led to improvement in soil and its yield. They used ash, poor quality corn, rotten fruit, blood and bones as manure to make their farms more fertile. Even ordinary farmers were able to produce manure while experts helped them create high quality varieties. They graded manure and used different varieties for different plants. They constructed cisterns for manufacturing fertilisers such that its stench did not offend anyone nor cause any wastage. They collected everything which could serve as an ingredient for manure.

A striking feature of the day was that modern methods were blended with conventional ones, which produced amazing results. Although there were many large farms, there was no feudal system or nobility who owned them. Rather, these were well managed on a small scale. The skills and labour of a family were involved in managing a farm. This family unit system planted human values and kinship in the agricultural life of the day.

Medieval Sind: Historians aptly observe that the Arabs, being inhabitants of a desert, were not favourably inclined towards agriculture. However, after conquering such fertile lands as Yemen, Egypt, Iraq and Syria, when they reached Sind, they left no stone unturned in transforming this largely arid place into an area fit for agriculture. As the Muslims had changed the topography of Andalusia after its conquest, they transformed Mehran into a fertile place. Apart from discovering new agricultural methods they planted fruit-bearing trees of coconut, mulberry, banana, mango and lemon. Moreover, they introduced the vegetables which were grown in other countries. Maize was regarded as a product exclusive to America. It was introduced later to Europe. Muslims started growing it in Sind. On account of their efforts, local people became familiar with new methods. Apart from other things, they planted trees along roads, streets and at public rest houses. It transformed the topography of the Sind. It became possible for people to raise cash crops. They drew up calendars for sowing in different seasons.

The Arabs also grafted grapes in the Sind and improved their taste. Likewise, they grafted the almond with the rose and as a result, better varieties of these plants were produced. They exported the seeds of the orange from Mansurah to Andalusia. The Arabs called it 'Naranj' and so it came to be known as 'orange' in Europe. They also exported tamarind from Sind to Iraq and transferred the juicy, fragrant olive from there. Lentils too, reached from Yemen to the South Asian subcontinent. The Muslim advent in Sind had an electrifying impact upon agriculture in Sind, because the local people came to know about many new plants and crops.

Persia: Agriculture was regarded in Persia as the key to prosperity. During the Islamic period this tradition continued. Muslim rulers spared no opportunity to promote it. In doing so, they ensured general prosperity in their kingdom. They therefore paid special attention to irrigation and the system of cultivation and to revenue collection. This put an end to the exploitation of farmers and lent stability to the sociopolitical order. Muslim scholars developed this discipline more as a modern industry.

Ottoman Caliphate: During the Ottoman Caliphate between the fourteenth to seventeenth centuries, freehold land was considered to be property of the Sultan. During the period of Caliph Sulayman I, it was the duty of the Sultan to maintain the data of freehold land which was reserved for farming. Whoever reclaimed land for farming was lavishly rewarded. Since the population was on the increase, the rulers encouraged higher yields. Special attention was paid to cultivating rice. This whole exercise was carried out under the supervision of the officials and relevant financial institutions concerned, who were responsible, in the main, for farming.

On studying Ottoman history, one learns that grain markets existed in every locality, which served as an incentive for higher yield. The surplus grain was exported to far-off lands by both land and sea routes. Venice imported in large quantities from Western Anatolia in the fifteenth Century. In particular, cotton and dry fruits were exported from Anatolia to northern regions.

In the sixteenth century and later, agricultural trade increased with Western Europe and cotton and its products were also exported to Eastern Europe. One of the reasons for this progress was that an efficacious irrigation system was in place even in the desert areas of the Muslim kingdom. Farming was carried out in the light of the latest agricultural research.

India: It emerges from reading *Aaeen-i-Akbari* and other documents of Aurangzeb's reign, that the land under cultivation was half of what it was at the beginning of this century. The vast area spread from Bihar, central and northern India to present day Pakistan. There were many large forests, for example in Rohilkhand in the thirteenth and fourteenth centuries, which were razed to the ground at a later date. It is worth mentioning that during Babur's reign, two methods were employed for drawing water: wooden pulleys and with the help of the bullock wheel. The latter attracted the king's special attention and he had vast cisterns built near rivers.

Many new crops were introduced during Muslim rule. Some important crops of today such as maize, potatoes, tea and peanuts were the order of that age. In terms of geographical features the crops were similar to what obtains now. Separate areas were earmarked then as now for growing wheat and rice. Jute was a highly profitable crop in most parts of Bengal. The silk worm industry, which is at present in decline, was then highly developed and silk worms were raised on a large scale in Bengal and Kashmir. During Mughal rule, India was so prosperous that it was known for its affluence throughout the world. Notwithstanding being a multi-faith and multi-ethnic country, it enjoyed peace and social cohesion, of which no parallel exists in the history of non-Muslims.

Acting on his gifted intelligence, Sher Shah Suri performed well as ruler. He entrusted village administration to local officials, ranging from security guards to land officials. His reform of the revenue system brought about tremendous progress in agriculture. He was on a par with 'Alauddin Khilji for accomplishing the measurement and registration of the entire land. He divided it into plots, which were given serial numbers and the entire division was recorded in registers. During his reign, the land revenue rate was fixed at one-third of the produce, which the farmer was free to give in cash or kind. He instructed officials to treat farmers kindly. However, no undue favour was to be shown them. Revenue was waived in the case of famine or other disasters. Loans were granted and stringent laws were enacted that prevented the exploitation of farmers at the hands of landlords. No official would dare accept bribery.

Akbar ordered the measurement of all agricultural land. While abandoning old units of measurement, he introduced new ones that could hardly be tampered with. His unit was 60 yards long and each yard was 33 inches long. Thus a *bigha* land comprised 3600 square yards. This record was faithfully preserved. His other major step was the classification of land into four categories in terms of its fertility. These were further subdivided into various categories. Akbar granted easy loans from the royal treasury to farmers so that they could improve the soil and install wells. These loans were to be repaid in easy instalments.

Irrigation System: Scarcity of water afflicted almost all parts of the Muslim world, from Sind to Morocco, with some notable exceptions. Accordingly such methods were developed which ensured the optimal use of even a little water. The techniques employed on this count transformed irrigation into technology. Muslims inherited various irrigation systems. However, they were not content with these. Apart from modernising them, they experimented with new methods. In Egypt, Muslims studied the tides of the Nile river, which helped solve many problems. Both Caliphs Mamun and al-Mutawakkil, had equipment erected on the river which is in operation even today and serves as a testament to the glory of Muslim scientists.

In Tanzania several dams were built on streams. Here, according to local circumstances, Muslim civil engineers designed these dams, which were constructed mainly with bricks and sand. These were so durable that they are operational even today. Some of these may be seen in North Africa. Their durability attests to the greatness of their builders. The water of these dams was used for both domestic and agricultural purposes. Cisterns were therefore constructed for connecting with rivers. A network of these dotted the landscape in Andalusia and Persia and in so doing Muslim scholars drew upon ancient Egyptian, Roman and Byzantine techniques. Muslims later introduced this system into India and it was highly popular during the Mughal period.

These Muslim achievements may be appreciated more in the light of their expertise in cartography and general skills. They drew upon their mathematical knowledge and other skills in bringing water to the desert towns from the mountain tops. At times they had to dig canals fifty feet deep and direct these upwards. Their success rested on their scientific and technological expertise and their devotion to knowledge. These achievements are a pointer to material progress, which forms a part of Islamic civilisation and of which the manifestations may be observed even today.

4.3 The Muslim Horticultural System

Inspired by the Qur'anic account of the Garden, Muslims developed the discipline of horticulture a great deal. In seventy-three verses of twenty-two Qur'anic chapters, reference is made to the gardens of Paradise. According to these verses there is an intrinsic link between one's good deeds and the gardens of Paradise. One will earn the reward of admission to the Garden, which embodies deliverance and peace. One will enjoy rivers, springs and comfort of every kind in Paradise.

Let us see the progress of horticulture in different Muslim countries during the medieval period.

Syria: Syria occupied the central position during the Umayyad period. It exhibits the glory of both Muslim horticulture and architecture. Umayyad Caliphs had palaces and hunting rest houses built outside the main towns and most of these had gardens attached. They also introduced the unique feature of reserving a sanctuary in which wild animals, deer, rabbits and ostrich lived. The area was properly fenced. Caliph Hisham built such a site in

729 CE. Walid I constructed a similar sanctuary in eastern Jordan between 712 and 715 CE.

Andalusia: When Muslims arrived in Andalusia, most of its land was barren and uninhabitable. There were no rivers or canals. Only places with an abundant natural water supply were fertile. However, some of these had been reduced to dreadful marshes on account of excess water. No one could cross these marshes. Professor Scott writes expressing his amazement at how desert-dwelling Arabs, ignorant of farming, turned into excellent town planners in Andalusia. There is nothing intriguing about it. For Arabs had abandoned their desert lifestyle more than a century previously. They had lived for long in fertile Syria. As a result they were skilled farmers when they arrived in Andalusia. Moreover, these migrants were industrious and built canals to promote farming. More remarkably, they created reservoirs on rivers to store water.

All the buildings constructed by the Umayyads for centuries in Andalusia had gardens attached to them. The Umayyads had a special fascination for flowers and greenery. As a result, they maintained evergreen gardens. The whole coastal area from Gibraltar to Barcelona looked like a vast garden. In the lower region of Seville (Ishbiliyah) there were gardens spread over miles of land. The valley of Almeria (al-Mariyah) was full of fruit and flowers over an area of forty miles. The district of Azardqa abounded in gardens. Keeping in mind the features of the local soil, Muslim rulers planted thousands of new saplings. More remarkably, plants from the whole world were grown there. Even herbs which grew only in the Himalayan region were exported and cultivated here industriously.

The practice of raising many crops in a year is popular these days. It was the Muslim experts in Andalusia who introduced this. They enriched their farms with a variety of fertilisers and reaped many crops. Unlike the farmers of other countries, they did not let their soil lie idle. After two months they raised another crop. On the sides of their farms they planted mulberry trees and raised silk worms in them and honeybees on their blossoms' nectar. They prepared pickles and cultivated precious herbs. All this resulted in higher income for them, enabling them to lead a comfortable life. The rural population during the Umayyad period was so prosperous that it was hard to come by a beggar or poor person.

The Umayyad rulers of Andalusia provided all facilities to farmers for ensuring a higher yield. They had canals constructed wherever it was possible to do so and dug ponds and wells at other places. The pond of al-Qanaat exists to this day and is three miles long and fifty feet deep. Moreover, they had numerous dams and embankments built that are in operation even today, around one thousand years after their construction.

The facilities provided to farmers in the Umayyad period were unprecedented. They enjoyed much freedom. They elected their own councils. Owing to their prosperity, there was hardly any need to grant them loans for raising crops. However, when some disaster struck them, the government offered them all possible help and no effort was spared in assisting them. The government had opened agricultural institutions, as part of its long term policy for development in districts and other towns. The children of farmers had ample facilities there for learning.

One of the factors of the phenomenal success of Muslims in horticulture in Andalusia was their mastery over botany. They were fully conversant with plant structure and their gender specific features. They knew how to graft and how to develop gardens. They were exceptionally good at flower decoration. Moreover, they were aware of the medicinal properties of plants. Apart from the nobles, the general public took a special interest in developing and maintaining gardens. The department of horticulture enjoyed state patronage. Delegates were sent to different parts of the world in order to collect samples of seeds and plants. There were special gardens for both local and exotic plants and the experiments carried out there were recorded in writing. It was amazing that whether in the oases of Asia or Africa, the green lands on the banks of the river Nile, the fertile plains of Iraq, the mountains of Central Asia or the Ganges plain, Cordoban scholars were engaged everywhere in enriching the subject of horticulture. It was due to their expertise that they were successful in producing apples the size of melons. They exported Andalusian mulberries to Baghdad and brought back Oriental fruits, such as lemons, date palms, figs, bananas, pomegranates, almonds and saffron.

Many towns in Andalusia were surrounded for miles by gardens, and visitors had to pass between fruit-bearing, shady trees. This account will, however, be incomplete without reference to the sprawling gardens and tall trees of Granada. This town appeared to be submerged in tall oak trees, grape vines and fruit trees. The town was so fertile that it is hard to describe its prosperity. The fruits, both fresh and dry, filled local shops the year round. Royal gardens, numbering more than one hundred, encircled the whole town. This valley, with its flowing canals, stood out for its charm and beauty. As snow melted and flowed into the lakes, and the shadows of tall trees and palaces were reflected in these, one thought of the exquisite beauty of Paradise. Local people thoroughly enjoyed these scenes. When they returned from work in the evening, they were refreshed by fragrant gardens.

Iraq: The city of Baghdad was founded by the Tigris river near the ancient town of Babil (Babylon) during the Abbasid period. Many gardens were built here. When the Caliph al-Mansur had his palace constructed, one of its main components was the garden. Court poets have praised the gardens of the Caliphs and nobles highly. The garden next to the palace of Asadullah was famous. He extended it further. The land bought for its extension was rocky, so first he had all the rocks removed and then replaced with fertile soil. Water-wheels were placed at the river for watering the garden. However, as this method could not provide enough water, he directed his engineers to build a canal for the garden. Accordingly it was constructed. Even elephants imported from India were used in the construction. Sultan Mahmud Ghaznavi had cordial relations with the Abbasid kingdom. Owing to this interaction, the latter's influence reached Khurasan and many gardens were erected there. Within a short time, Ghazna turned into a town dotted with palaces and gardens. This trend continued and influenced those under Ghaznavi rule.

Egypt: Arab civilisation reached a zenith in Egypt during the reign of Fatimid Caliphs. Owing to the general prosperity, the fertile lands and trade links, the Egyptian Caliphs were richer than those of Baghdad. Most of their wealth was spent on trade and industry, luxury items and the construction of palaces and inns. Special mention is made in works of history of the garden built by the Fatimid Caliph al-Mustansir, of which the ground, beds, trees, fruits, and leaves were made of gold and precious stones. One of its tents was two hundred metres in diameter and twenty-eight metres high. It was made of brocade, resting on six pillars of silver. At a much earlier date, during the reign of the Abbasid Caliph, al-Muqtadir Billah had a magnificent artificial tree in his court. When the Russian ambassador called on him he was overawed on witnessing it. This tree was at the centre of a pool and made of silver, weighing the equivalent of five hundred thousand dirhams. It had eighteen branches and each branch had many leaves. Birds made of gold and silver perched on this tree and as the breeze blew, the birds sang in melodious tunes.

Morocco: The Moroccan rulers constructed many palaces enclosed in lush green lawns and gardens which were on the Andalusian models. After the decline of Marinid rule, these gardens were deserted. However during the reign of the 'Alawi Sultan Mawlay 'Abd ar-Rahman (1824-1834), these were restored. The Sultan also built a large garden, containing both local and exotic varieties of flowers. Lakes flowed midst trees and visitors sailed on boats. The streams filling these lakes catered also for gardens and windmills. The archaeological dig at the earliest mosque in al-Katbiya in Morocco has brought into relief the outline of a small garden which was erected in the days of 'Ali ibn Yusuf al-Marabuti (1106-1142). It was rectangular and had flower-beds on all sides. Ahmad Mansuri Asa'di (1578-1603) adopted the Alhambra school of horticulture in his place in Morocco. It had a courtyard 135 metres long and 110 metres wide, with rooms and galleries on all sides.

Iran: Persian life was influenced by Abbasid culture and a hallmark of Persian gardens during Muslim rule was that everyone, the rich and the poor alike had gardens attached to their homes, containing fruit bearing trees and flowers. The rich had enclosed gardens with flowing streams. In the fifteenth century, the Safavids replaced Timur's dynasty, yet they maintained the patronage of gardens. When Shah Abbas chose Isfahan as his capital, he ordered many gardens in the city. He was specially attracted towards gardens. Some of his famous gardens are Chahar Bagh, Hasht Bihisht and Chahal Sutoon.

India: Prior to the coming of Islam in India, gardens did not enjoy any special place in life there. However, when Muslims gained control of the region, they built houses, palaces, forts and, for decoration and beauty, they planted trees and plants. This led to the development of gardens. Before Mughal rule, the gardens built by earlier Muslim rulers were in a state of neglect. They renovated these and planted trees, water falls and fountains. They planted in these trees from hilly regions, which flourish up to this day. It goes without saying that the Mughals transformed the landscape of this region. In their works, Amir Khusro and Malik Muhammad Jaisi have described at length the flora and fauna of the region. Muslims introduced many flowers such as banafsha, yasmeen, nasreen, bela, kewra, champa, mulsari, suyuti, damra, karna and gul-i-sad barg.

Akbar had Naseem Bagh built besides the lake of Dal. It was the oldest garden of Kashmir, some of the trees still surviving since the planting of this garden. Experts think that the Chinar trees were planted during Shah Jahan's reign, for it was his distinguished engineer 'Ali Mardan Khan who introduced this tree in India. In addition to Kashmir, the Mughals had gardens built in other parts of India. The floating garden in the Jamuna river by Humayun is of special note. For it was decked on floating wooden boxes. The mausoleum built by Shah Jahan in memory of his beloved wife Mumtaz Mahal known as Taj Mahal is universally recognised as one of the wonders of the world. A large garden forms part of this complex - equally attractive are its flower beds, pools and canals. The beauty of the Taj Mahal is dependent largely upon its garden.

It must be clarified that Muslim rulers' interest in gardens did not reflect their personal inclination. These gardens were not reserved exclusively for royal families. On the contrary, their doors were open to everyone in order to make the public aware of natural beauty and to appreciate fruits, flowers, trees and scenic attractions. The promotion of the garden led also to the resurgence of poetry and literature, painting, music, spirituality and religious consciousness. Poets, painters and Sufis drew inspiration, imagination and spiritual lessons from gardens. In a sense, these gardens played a role as important as those of libraries and educational institutions.

4.4 Agricultural Research and Publications

Muslims' special interest in agriculture can also be judged from their research and publications in the field. During the golden centuries of Islamic civilisation, Muslim scientists carried out new experiments in the field. More importantly, they recorded their observations. It would not be an exaggeration to say that their works were most comprehensive in their coverage. These works were truly encyclopaedic, devoted fully to the discipline of agriculture. These deal with various types of soil, features of water and fertilisers, methods of growing crops, precautionary measures for raising fruit-bearing trees, grafting, land measurement, zoology, the honeybee and raising a host of animals. Experts in the field, workers, farmers and gardeners cooperated with one another in the production of these works. Since it was an essentially scientific activity to write on agriculture, scholars studied plants in a detailed manner. Physicians studied these from a medicinal angle. Given below is an account of the major works in the field carried out in various geographical regions.

Far West: Muslims enjoyed a monopoly in certain fields of study. Agriculture in Andalusia offers its brightest example. A careful study shows that Arab and Spanish writings on agriculture bore many striking features. 'Abdullah ibn Bassal was an agricultural scientist. Ibn Wafid was basically a physician while Ibn Bajjah an orator and imam, and Ibn Lawyun a distinguished poet, yet all of them attained fame on account of their special interest in agriculture. It was the time when the radiance of light emanating from Muslim Cordoba, Granada and Almeria illuminated the academic world far and wide. Books and journals on agriculture published from Andalusia played a key role in academic progress and critical enquiry.

The oldest work in Arabic on the subject is Ibn Wahshiyah's *Al-Filahat an-Nabatiya*, which was written in 904 CE. At a later date Qustus ibn Saqar Sakinah's *Al-Filahat ar-Rumiyyah* came out. These works were later pop popd into other languages. Of all the books written by Abu 'Umar ibn Hajjaj, his *Kitab al-Muqanna* gained much fame. His contemporary, 'Abdullah ibn Bassal of Toledo visited all of Muslim Spain, north Africa and the Arabian peninsula. On his return to Spain he wrote his comprehensive book *Diwan al-Filahah*. His other work was *Kitab al-Qasd wa'l-Bayan*. Both these works were based on his wide-ranging personal observations. Included in these are discussions on the medicinal value of plants, different types of water and their use for irrigation purposes. Ibn Bassal had a special interest in soil and its types in relation to agricultural yield. This aspect features prominently in his books. In 1085 CE, he applied his theoretical knowledge to building a garden in Seville at the command of its Muslim ruler, Mu'tamid ibn 'Abbas.

Muhammad ibn Malik of Granada was a great writer on the subject. His fourteen-volume work *Zahrat al-Bustan wa Nuzhat al-Adhan* is on plant agronomy. To attain expertise in the field, he undertook a long journey. On his visit to Seville he had a very fruitful meeting with Ibn Bassal and drew on the latter's experience.

Numerous works on the subject were produced in Andalusia from the tenth century onwards. Abu'l Hasan's *Kitab al-Anwa'* also features an agricultural calendar. Abu'l-Qasim Zahrawi benefited much from it in writing his *Kitab al-Filahah*. His student Abd ar-Rahman ibn Wafid, head of the royal garden in Toledo, also wrote a book, with the same title, which was highly popular in Islamic lands and elsewhere. It was pop popd into various languages. Moreover, it served as the basis for later writings on the subject. Among the twelfth century's Muslim agricultural scientists, Abu'l-Khayr al-Ishbili stands out. His work *Kitab al-Filahah* is preserved as a manuscript in libraries in Paris, Tunis and North Africa. It contains a wealth of information on crops, fruit bearing plants, vegetables, flower insects, pests and animals. Abu Zakariyya Yahya ibn Muhammad's masterpiece *Kitab al-Filahah* is not only a major work of Muslim Andalusia but of its age. Comprising thirty-four chapters, this book was devoted, in the main, to agriculture, for its first thirty chapters were on this subject. The rest dealt with raising cattle, poultry and honeybees. This work was pop popd into Turkish, French, Spanish and Urdu.

Middle East: It emerges from the contents of Muslim works on agriculture, that these experts were highly skilled in recording their observations. Most of the works dealt with artificial fertilisers, agricultural tools, plantation, irrigation, crops and plant preservation, etc. These related the many improvements and advances in the field. Contained in them also were extensive discussions on legumes and cereals and their effects on soil. It is worth mentioning that in addition to Muslim scholars of the day, Muslim rulers too, had a special interest in the subject. Two thirteenth century rulers of Yemen, 'Umar ibn Yusuf and 'Abbas ibn 'Ali contributed books and monographs on the subject. The latter is known for his work namely *Baghithat al-Filahin fi Ashjar-i-Thamari wa'r-Riyahin*. At the same time Ibn Mamati compiled his *Qawanin ad-Dawawin* which was reprinted in 1943 by the Royal Agricultural Society, Cairo. In the next century, Jamal ad-Din Watwat (d. 1318) produced *Mubahith al-Fikr wa Manahij al-Birr*, of which volume four was on agriculture and botany.

Although there was a marked decrease in the number of Muslim publications on agriculture from the sixteenth century onwards, a significant work was Qasim ibn Yusuf Abi Ansari's *Irshad az-Zahrat*. His contemporary, Riaz ad-Din Ghazi Almeiri was also credited with a major work on the subject. In the seventeenth century, al-Hajj Ibrahim ibn Ahmad wrote in Turkish his *Rawnaq-i-Bustan* and Kamani his *Ghars Namah*. In the next century, Sufi 'Abd al-Ghani an-Nabalusi (d. 1731) produced his *'Alam al-Milahah fi 'Ilm al-Filahah*, which was published in Damascus.

India: It goes without saying that those who engaged in agriculture were more interested in practical than theoretical knowledge of the subject. For them agriculture was essentially an applied science. Although their expertise was reflected in their writings to a degree, the exact range of this applied science was difficult to measure only in terms of their books. Most of this knowledge was preserved in memory, which was expressed best in mutual exchange of views. Yet in the Islamic world, both spoken and written modes were used for the promotion of this field.

On studying the history of the subcontinent, it becomes fairly clear that Muslims accomplished so much in the field that its impact is evident even today. Both *Babar Nama* and *Tasneef-e-Ganj Abad* of Aman Ullah Hussaini (d. 1637), dealt in part with the subject. Apart from containing some valuable information, these described the prices and revenue rates of agricultural products in several provinces during Akbar's reign. They also delved deep into the data on agricultural land and irrigation systems. Some other works on the subject have, however, been lost. During Muslim rule, agriculture reached new heights. Muslims made advances in gardening, cultivation and irrigation. Their knowledge was nonetheless more than that documented in the works of the day.

5.
Social Sciences and other Disciplines

During the middle period, Muslims manufactured high quality paper which was used for disseminating works by leading scholars, writers, and teachers. As in other disciplines, Muslims were accomplished masters in shipbuilding and navigation. In the early Islamic period, the Muslim fleet had 1700 ships. This number increased and played an important role in the expansion of global trade.

5.1 History and Sociology

In the early Islamic days, historical works were concerned in the main with providing an account of the Prophet's life ﷺ. Hisham ibn 'Abd al-Malik was the first author to pop pop a book from a foreign language into Arabic. At a later date, there appeared on the scene, many eminent Muslim historians who recounted events which had been largely forgotten. By the fourth Islamic century Hijrah, history was developed as a substantial discipline by Muslims. A team of historians attended the Abbasid court. Ibn Ahmad Ya'qub and Ahmad ibn Yahya al-Baladhuri were the leading historians of this era. They added much to the subject. Two of Baladhuri's works enjoyed worldwide fame.

Of all the renowned Muslim historians who made lasting contributions, Ibn Khaldun (d. 1406) stands out above others. His epoch-making work was spread over several volumes. With his command of social sciences and his deep study of nature, he developed the subject along definite lines. He laid the foundations of social studies as a science. Impressed by his scholarly approach Colosio states that Ibn Khaldun presented for the first time in his *Muqaddimah* the concept of historical evolution. He took into consideration climatic and geographic conditions and moral and spiritual values which have a bearing upon history. He was no doubt the founder of social sciences. With his *Muqaddimah*, he introduced sociology as an independent subject. There is a consensus on the point that Ibn Khaldun is the most accomplished Muslim historian and will always be remembered as an eminent philosopher. Even before Ibn Khaldun, Muslims had established their credentials as historians. Al-Mas'udi (d. 965) travelled to almost every country in Asia and produced the first work on world history in thirty volumes.

At-Tabari (from Persia) used to write daily, approximately forty pages and his book on history runs into thirty volumes. He visited

Persia and Egypt and during his journey he faced at times such harsh conditions that he had to sell all that he had. Yet he went ahead consistently with his academic pursuits. Ibn Hayyan also contributed as many as fifty books on the history of Spain. Abu'l-Faraj (d. 967) wrote in twenty-one volumes his history of Arabic poetry. Al-Biruni was the first to lay down the principles of historiography. Ibn al-Khatib (d. 1376), a historian of Muslim Spain produced sixty books on a variety of subjects. Ibn Khallikan contributed an account of the leading figures of Muslim history. Nicholson regards it as the best specimen of historiography. Ibn Battutah, a world traveller (d. 1377), is an internationally renowned figure. Although he was not a historian, his travelogue on medieval Indian history is a rich mine of information.

In addition to the above, several Muslim historians are remembered. There were many factors which led to the promotion of history as a subject by Muslims. One of these was geography and the list of towns. For studying hadith and other subjects, Muslim students travelled from one town to another and visited many countries. Their need for this travelling was one of the important factors which encouraged them to learn history and geography. Apart from recording history, Muslim scholars preserved accounts of 600,000 *Ulama* (Muslim religious scholars).

5.2 Philosophy

During the glorious middle period of Islam, no branch of learning was neglected. Muslim scholars were equally interested in all subjects. A chemist or astronomer could be a first-rate philosopher as well. An instance in point is 'Umar Khayyam; in the West his fame rests on being a poet and philosopher. However, he was also a distinguished mathematician and astronomer. Likewise, Ibn Khaldun was a historian, philosopher and chronicler at the same time. Philip Hitti writes that he was the greatest historian and philosopher produced by Islam, and will be remembered in all ages. Another Muslim scholar, whose interest was not confined to science, was the physician Ibn Rushd. Hitti speaks of him thus: the physician in Ibn Rushd overwhelmed the philosopher that existed in him. A French scholar records that Islam, in the light of its contribution to linguistics and history, is a rational faith, which is rooted in such principles characterised by reason and logic.

Muslims did not commence their studies of science with an unconventional philosophy; yet their contributions to the field are solid and of immense significance. They presented solutions to philosophical problems which were acceptable to that age. They paved the way for further studies and facilitated the revival of knowledge in Europe. This contribution places them in an elevated position in the history of philosophy. Some of the eminent Muslim philosophers are 'Umar Khayyam, Ibn Rushd, al-Kindi with 263 books to his credit, al-Farabi, the author of more than one hundred books, Ibn Miskawayh, who anticipated Darwin's theory of evolution some nine centuries earlier, Ibn Sina who elucidated a concept of evolution, and Ibn al-Haytham, Ibn Bajah and Ibn at-Tufayl. What prompted Muslims to undertake the study of philosophy were the Qur'anic ayat which exhort Muslims to reflect on natural phenomena. They were told that there are divine signs for those who reflect.

5.3 Law and Independent Judiciary

The most significant Muslim contribution to law is that they made the judiciary independent of the executive. The Caliphs themselves set an example on this count. Whenever they were called, they surrendered themselves to the judiciary like any ordinary citizen. When there was a case of litigation between Caliph 'Umar and Ibn Abi Ka'b, the reigning Caliph Umar appeared as an ordinary citizen before Zayd ibn Thabit's court. The Qadi (judge) vacated his chair as a mark of respect for the Caliph. However, the Caliph took it as contrary to the spirit of justice and sat along with the other party. Similarly, a case was registered against

Caliph Mansur and he appeared before the Qadi. Another case arose in the day of Caliph Mamun. While maintaining the supremacy of law he took his seat along with the accuser in court. The Prophet Muhammad ﷺ instructed Muslims to follow both the letter and spirit of the law strictly. He told them that earlier nations had been destroyed because they used to spare the rich and punish the poor.

On studying history one notes that law is generally based on local custom and ritual. The practices followed by a particular family or tribe came to be known later as law. In contrast, Islamic law is rooted in divine legislation and it does not admit any bias or the inclinations of a family or tribe. The main sources of Islamic law are: i) Qur'an, ii) *Sunnah* (acts of the Prophet ﷺ and of his rightly guided Caliphs), iii) consensus , iv) analogy, v) custom, and, vi) expediency. On the basis of these principles, the judiciary came into existence during the days of the Rightly Guided Caliphs. As already stated, it was kept independent of the executive which helped make it more efficient, autonomous and powerful. Free and prompt justice was ensured. Strict criteria were applied to the appointment of the Chief Justice. Only a first-rate scholar who combined piety and justice could be considered for this position. At times, even some practical tests were conducted in order to ensure the highest possible standard of appointment. It is noteworthy, that in this modern time, in most of the countries of the world, there is no department to inform the general public of state laws and regulations. However, the department of *Ifta* in the days of Muslim Caliphs discharged this duty so that an ordinary citizen would not face any hardship in securing justice. As in the judiciary, much care was exercised in appointing officials in this department.

5.4 Literature and Poetry

All the great Muslim scholars and teachers of the middle period of Islam put their discoveries into writing for the benefit of others. Muslims were masters at manufacturing the high quality paper used for writing books. Many booksellers were engaged in supplying books to hundreds of thousands of avid readers. Their devotion to the book industry was indicative of their concern for the promotion of knowledge. Muslims' major contributions to the academic and literary fields are common knowledge. They were adept also in composing poetry. Even in pre-Islamic Arabia, poetry was highly popular. The Prophet ﷺ patronised literary activities.

Phillip Hitti has discussed at length the impact Islamic and Arabic men of letters had on Europe and the influence of Arabic on Western literary masterpieces. Similar views have also been expressed by Lane Poole, who says that in Europe, poetry never evoked the interest of ordinary people. In contrast, people of every social class composed poetry in Andalusia. Their poetical accomplishments were emulated in Europe by poets and singers. No Andalusian speaker was content with his speech unless he could compose couplets on the spot as part of his oration - or he could, at least, recite a master's couplet in his speech.

Poetry is of special importance in the academic and literary life of any community, and Arabic poetry exhibits a vast range. The Arabs were experts in eloquence and rhetoric. No nation could rival them on this count. Knowledge in general and literature and poetry in particular received a boost in the days of Caliph Harun ar-Rashid. This patronage endured for a long time. Literature reached new heights during this period. The Caliph was such a generous patron of learning that he lavishly rewarded those who pop popd literary texts into Arabic.

5.5 Political System and Governance

It is common knowledge that Islam prescribes consultation. However, the little known truth about Islamic polity is that the right to legislate rests only with Allah. An individual or a group of persons are not authorised to issue laws. Allah alone enjoys this prerogative. However, this does not imply that Islam entrusts political authority to clergy. Rather Muslims are granted a limited political freedom in the framework of the sovereignty of Allah. This represents theocracy in a consultative set up. Islam does not sanction dictatorship exercised by an individual or a group. The appointment of the ruler is on the basis of mutual consultation and consensus among the leading members of the Muslim society.

The Prophet ﷺ laid the foundation of the Islamic polity and later it gained in extent and detail. New departments were set up for a better functioning of governance and to ensure public welfare. It was Caliph 'Umar who established for the first time departments corresponding in some of their duties to police and public works. The Caliph established his rule and his passing of legal judgements on the basis of his consultation with eminent Companions.

It is worth mentioning regarding polity and governance, that when the Prophet ﷺ established the first Islamic community in Madinah, it attained such remarkable success within ten years that grain wasn't imported. Rather, surplus grain was, on occasion, exported. The polity established by the Messenger of Allah ﷺ existed on four levels: local, district, divisional and provincial. In other words, a highly efficient mode, covering the entire range from lower to higher tiers, was introduced. All decisions were taken with adequate consultation with qualified and expert people. This way had been so well established that when the mode of governance changed from Caliphate into monarchy, the system of administration continued along the traditional lines.

5.6 Navigation and Shipbuilding

The tradition of navigation and shipbuilding has been reported in Islam since the days of the Prophet Nuh, peace be upon him. He had built an ark at Allah's command in order to save the lives of the believers. During the Caliph Mu'awiyah's reign, the Muslim fleet comprised 1700 ships. By the days of the Caliph Harun ar-Rashid, Muslim rule had spread from central Asia to northwest Africa and Tariq ibn Ziyad had won Spain. The Muslim navy reigned supreme in the Mediterranean and Atlantic oceans and their ships made trade voyages all over the world. A trade centre flourished in the port of Mindnigo on the western coast of Africa. The language used in this town contained many Arabic words employed for carrying out trade. Some of this vocabulary reached the American state, Michouean. American local dialects absorbed some of these Arabic words by this route.

An article on Muslim culture in Spain appeared in *Ma'arif* (vols. 5: 6-7). It was written by Raphael, who was a director of higher education and professor in Madrid University. The article contained quotations from *Cambridge Medieval History*. For Raphael, the Muslim fleet in Spain attained its glory during the reign of 'Abd al-'Adil and during that time Almeria served as an important port for the export of cotton and other items.

It is noteworthy that Columbus is credited with the discovery of America and everything related to the 'new-world' is dated from his expedition. Some historians argue that, in fact, America had been discovered much before 1492. Historical records suggest that a French traveller had reached Brazil in 1489. He was guided by a Spanish sailor. In 1492 the same sailor and his two brothers accompanied Columbus. In his report, Columbus acknowledges that on arriving in America he discovered black Africans. They were obviously the descendants of the African Muslims who had introduced words from the Arabic language, elements of Islamic civilisation and Middle Eastern plants to the eastern coasts of South America. As mentioned earlier, during their glorious period, the Islamic navy dominated all the sea routes. At that time in South America, the Aztec and Mayan civilisations flourished. These civilisations resembled the Arab-African civilisation. It may, therefore, be inferred safely that Muslims had discovered America before Columbus [see *Deeper Roots* by Abdullah Hakim Quick, Ta-Ha Publishing Ltd., London, 1996, for more details, since a great deal of evidence has arisen on this topic]. Moreover, they had trade links with it. They hold the credit also for exporting the cotton of the old world to America. Thanks to this the American and Egyptian varieties appeared which are now found everywhere.

It is a historical truth that when a nation is defeated on the battleground, it is gradually relegated to backwardness in all spheres of life. It cannot encounter even the academic onslaught of the victors. In every age the thought of the victorious and ruling nation dominates. Little wonder then that Western thinkers dominate the scene today. Their writings suppress the truth. However, there are a few Western scholars who are not a party to hiding truth. Regarding the naval voyages undertaken by Muslims, one Western scholar says that some adventurous sailors had reached American shores six hundred years before Columbus. When Phillip III expelled the Muslims from Spain, they set up a naval base in 1661 in Morocco. Sailors were instructed there. They were trained to organise fleets.

In the days of the Ottoman Caliphate, a grand naval fleet was set up in order to defend islands and ships from pirates and crusaders. Admiral [*Amir al-Bahr* – amir of the sea] Khayr ad-Din Barbarossa was entrusted with this responsibility. Drawing upon his enormous skills and strategic abilities, he defended Muslim ports and coasts for many years against the enemy. Moreover, the Ottomans set up shipbuilding yards and training centres.

Ibn Majid holds pride of place in the history of Muslim shipping. He compiled material on its history. In 1489, he produced his book *al-Fawa'id fi Usul al-'Ilm al-Jari wa'l-Qawa'id*, comprising twelve chapters. Included were descriptions of sea routes and ports. Of Ibn Majid's thirty-two works, *Hadiyat al-Ikhtisar fi Usul al-Bihar, al-'Arabiyyah Qiblat al-Islam fi Jami'i ad-Dunya* and *Arjuzatu Birr al-'Arab fi Khalij al-Faras* deserve special mention. In 1498, when Vasco da Gama arrived at a place on the eastern coast of Africa on his way to India, he was guided by Ibn Majid to his destination. Some Portuguese historians have described this event. Many of them recognise Ibn Majid as the master of shipping.

Some European scholars credit the Chinese with the invention of the compass. However, George Sarton, Phillip Hitti and R.F. Burton consider it a Muslim invention. They hold that Muslim sailors of the 10th and 11th centuries should be ranked equal with Columbus. Here, with reference to the context, it will be of some interest to readers, that during Caliph 'Umar's ruler (in the early period of Islamic history), the Egyptian Governor 'Amr ibn al-'As had submitted a feasibility report to the Caliph on the construction of a canal joining the Red Sea with the Mediterranean. Since Muslims of the day did not have enough naval power, and apprehensive of naval attacks by the Greeks, they did not act on the Suez canal plan. However, a huge canal was built joining the river Nile with the Red Sea.

5.7 Architecture

Islamic architecture originated in Damascus. All decorative devices not forbidden by Shari'ah were adopted. Islamic architecture was displayed first in mosques with impressive arches. When Banu Abbas (the Abbasids) took over the reins of power from Banu Umayyah (the Umayyads), Umayyad architecture had reached Andalusia and Egypt. Even after Baghdad became the capital, Umayyad architecture flourished in North Africa and Andalusia. Later on, Berber and Moorish styles were also incorporated into it. For three centuries Cordoba and Granada followed the same pattern of Umayyad architecture. Mosques and palaces built in this period stand out for their alluring beauty. Islamic norms were faithfully followed in architecture. It was in the Umayyad period that Muslims constructed for the first time, magnificent mosques. Europeans were struck with awe on visiting these structures.

The West exhibits a marked influence from Muslim architecture. A living testament to it is the Cordoba mosque, a religious site. A non-religious site is the palace of Ishbiliyah (Seville) which bears out the beauty and splendour of Islamic architecture. It is akin to the interior design of the Alhambra (*al-Hamra* – the Red) palace of Granada. As a result of the Crusades, the Western and Islamic style of architecture became closer. A mixture of these is evident in Andalusia.

Tobakht (d. 776) was an accomplished engineer and architect. His role in the architecture of the new capital, Baghdad, was reflective of Muslim classical mastery. Various buildings in Egypt display Muslim expertise in architecture, especially of the skilled masters who had migrated to Egypt in the wake of the Mongol invasion of Damascus and Baghdad. Philip Hitti remarks on the splendour of Islamic architecture. He reveals that the domes were built in such a manner that one is left marvelling at their exquisite, fine quality and outward beauty. This design stands out above arches and other decorative devices. Two other prominent features were Eclidic Arab marks and calligraphy.

5.8 Painting

Although art is a contested subject in Islam, some Muslim artists did enrich the subject. Many public baths in Syria had walls with magnificent paintings. In the palaces of Walid (715-705) and Yazid II (720-724), paintings symbolised victory, poetry and philosophy. Many works of the nineteenth century, especially story books and textbooks on science contained illustrations of these works. Yahya ibn Ali, a leading artist of the day, is often cited.

During the middle period, illustrated books were common in India. Some royal books had coloured illustrations with golden borders. Today, many such works adorn museums in Lahore and Peshawar. During the Mughal period, Muslim artists produced several masterpieces. According to a chronicler, there were 24,000 manuscripts in the Agra library, many of these being illustrated with golden borders. Golden binding attained perfection during Muslim rule. The most ornate and well produced were the copies of the Qur'an.

Muslim artists of the Mughal era were experts in Indo-Persian painting. This discipline was promoted mainly in Rajputana, and local Muslims displayed their talents in a variety of ways. Some samples may be seen even today in the palaces and libraries in Jaipur. Muslims were so gifted that they vastly improved and enriched every discipline.

5.9 Oratory

Oratory has been an inextricable part of Islamic culture. From very early days, public announcements were made in mosques. For centuries, Muslim imams, scholars and students developed such skills and devices that could leave an imprint on the minds and hearts of their audience. The art of oratory had its beginning in delivering *khutbahs*. Gradually, it assumed the form of an independent discipline of literature. Oratory played an important role in the period when speeches were much more common and important than the written word.

During the Umayyad Caliphate, oratory was developed in an unprecedented way. It could not be surpassed in subsequent ages. Imams relied on oratory for conveying the deen in the Friday Prayers. Rulers and military generals drew upon it for infusing courage and loyalty in the Muslims. At a time when there was no propaganda machinery, oratory was the only means for disseminating views and thoughts. The sermons of Caliph 'Ali, may Allah be pleased with him, are characterised by rhetorical skills and wisdom. During the period of Harun ar-Rashid, this discipline registered further advances. The style became even more forceful, effective and sweeter. The introduction and presentation of new thought patterns enriched it further. It goes without saying that the Muslims excelled in this particular branch, for they had full command over eloquence, rhetorical skills and devices and possessed a grand and sombre style.

5.10 Educational Institutions and Libraries

In the early days of Islam, mosques also served as educational institutions. However, as the number of students greatly increased, independent educational institutions were founded. Ross and Rabera state that most children in the Muslim world had equal educational opportunities. In that period it was a common practice on the part of rulers, princes and the nobility to patronise learning and to open new educational institutions. As a result, there were numerous such institutions in every part of the Muslim world and the great majority of people were literate. There were large universities in Muslim Spain in the towns of Cordoba, Seville, Malaga and Granada. European scholars visited them to quench their thirst for knowledge. Many mosques, observatories, hospitals, literary and academic centres and private institutions also imparted education to students.

The educational movement reached its zenith during the Abbasid period under the patronage of the caliphs, especially during the reign of Harun ar-Rashid. There were hundreds of scribes in Baghdad alone and their works were bought at high prices. Paper manufacturing was a household industry in that period. This contributed much to the promotion of knowledge, literature and libraries. Libraries served also as educational centres. There were over 400,000 books in Cordoba library. Likewise, there was the staggering number of three and two million books in Tripoli (Lebanon) and Bayt al-Hikmah (Cairo) libraries, respectively. In Baghdad, Hormuz, Ray, Balkh and Ghazna too, there existed large libraries.

During the Sultanate period in Muslim India, Tughlaq had very cordial relations with Egypt. In his *Subh al-A'asha*, Qalqashandi has provided an account of Arab travellers to India who reported that during Tughlaq's rule, there were nearly one thousand educational institutions in Delhi. About Firoz Shahi Madrassa, the historian Ziauddin Barni states that in terms of its splendour and glory, location and beauty, and its administrative and academic excellence that it was the best madrasah. Royal stipends catered for its expenses. The Mughal period was also a golden age of knowledge and learning. Akbar issued the directive that learning be promoted at all costs so that the world be not devoid of masters and their contributions preserved.

One learns from Abu'l-Fadl's *A'aeen-e-Akbari* that students interested in higher studies went to the bigger cities in order to take lessons at the feet of distinguished scholars. The syllabus of the day comprised units of study on morals, agriculture, geometry, revenue, physics and history. The Mughal king Jahangir had issued a decree that the estate of an heirless person be set-aside for educational purposes.

Aurangzeb established numerous educational institutions. A traveller of that period, Alexander Hamilton, describes that there were four hundred educational institutions in Thatha, a town in Sind. Teachers, both Muslim and non-Muslim, received salaries from the public treasury. Even during the period of decline of Muslim rule, there were 80,000 educational institutions in Bengal. There was a school for every forty persons.

As already stated, arrangements were made from the early days of Islam for providing education to everyone. Apart from religious instruction, secular and technical education were also imparted. Some of the important departments of study were linguistics, commerce, medicine, industry, agriculture and other technical subjects. Specialisation was accessible for those interested.

5.11 Calligraphy

Muslims had such refined artistic taste that they developed calligraphy beyond recognition. They used it for decorative purposes. Generally speaking, nations are concerned only with the script of their language. However, Muslims improved upon every style of calligraphy. It became an inseparable part of Islamic culture and came to be known as one of the fine arts. An artist's creativity is central to both painting and calligraphy. Prompted by their Islamic ideals, Muslim artists introduced new ideas and styles. Little wonder then that one notes a wide range of designs. The first prominent figure in the field was Khalid ibn Abi Hayyaj.

Islamic calligraphy lent greater beauty to architecture. This art developed much with the passage of time. With the help of numerous colour combinations, the art of calligraphy appeared more and more captivating. For centuries, the Muslim masters worked very hard and the fruits of their labour adorn mosques, palaces, pottery and other decorative items. Even among the masters of this art in our times are Sadiqeen, Zubi, Aslam Kamal, 'Abd al-Wahid, Naheed al-Qum and Shafeeq Farooqi. With the strokes of their pen and brush they portray Islamic truths. Their efforts have enriched the subject further.

6.
Review and Reflections

Internally weak, relatively backward, frustrated, conflict-ridden, suffering from internal tensions, and often controlled and abused by foreign powers, the Muslim world is in a state of crisis. For Muslims, all modern history is a tragedy. At an earlier time, during the sweeping emergence of Islam, Muslims were the custodians of civilisation and both the centre and masters of the civilisation. But at present, the Muslim polity is neither master nor partner, and both Muslims and Islam are often regarded in world politics as little more than problematic. How did such a state of affairs come about, and in what ways can the Muslim peoples alter this condition? (AbdulHamid A. Abu Sulayman, *Towards an Islamic Theory of International Relations*)

6.1 Factors for the Rise and Fall of Muslims

It is widely believed in the Muslim world that Islam signifies progress and development. When Muslims neglect their faith, they fail to attain any success. Islam stands for global unity. In the Islamic philosophy, irrespective of their geographical locations, Muslims belong to one single community, i.e., the *Ummah*. Apart from laying down unity in faith, it gives the human being a comprehensive code of life governing social, moral and worldly life. Islam caters for human spiritual and moral needs and does not ignore any aspect of day-to-day life. For it is concerned with the overall welfare and progress of humankind. According to A.J. Arberry (late Professor of Arabic, University of Cambridge), it is obligatory to thank the Muslims who are the benefactors of humanity. The advances made by Muslims in numerous branches of learning are common knowledge. They could not have attained these achievements, if they had not been devoted to knowledge. Love for learning was their outstanding feature. Both Muslim men and women religiously followed the Prophet's ﷺ directive that they should seek knowledge, even if they had to travel to China for this purpose. The Islamic principles of education, their methodology and their studies make very interesting reading.

Due to the limited scope, it is beyond the reach of this book to discuss in detail various reasons for the rise and fall of Muslims in the middle period of history. However, one of the most important reasons for their success was their following a concept closer to the modern concept of human development, rather than the emphasis on economic growth. Thus, their main emphasis was on the development of the general public rather than a specific group of the society. What is the concept of human development? How did it develop? Why is it so important? And, what is its relation to the Muslim world? These are the questions that arise in the mind. To explore the answers to these questions, we need to discuss the philosophy and historical backgrounds of this type of approach to development.

Study of contemporary literature indicates that the World Bank was the first institution which adopted the concept of human development. In its *World Development Report 1980*, the Bank says: '...human resources development, here called human development to emphasize that it is an end as well as a means of economic progress. Human development encompasses education and training, better health and nutrition ... The case of human development is not only, or even primarily, an economic one. Less hunger, fewer child deaths and a better chance of primary education are almost universally accepted as important ends in themselves.' After a decade, in 1990, the concept of human development was refined somewhat and was adopted by the United Nations Development Programme (UNDP). In its first issue of *Human Development Report 1990*, the UNDP argued: 'Human development is a process of enlarging people's choices. The most critical of these wide-ranging choices are to live a long and healthy life, to be educated and to have access to resources needed for a decent standard of living.' *Human Development Report 1995*, advocates this concept as follows:

> The concept of human development is much broader than the conventional theories of economic development. Economic growth models deal with expanding GNP rather than enhancing the quality of human lives. Human resources development treats human beings primarily as an input in production process - a means rather than an end. Welfare approaches look at human beings as beneficiaries and not as agents of change in the development process. The basic-need approach focuses on providing material goods and services to deprived population groups rather than on enlarging human choices in all fields.

Human development, by contrast, brings together the production and distribution of commodities and the expansion and use of human capabilities. Encompassing these earlier concerns, human development goes beyond them. It analyses all issues in society - whether economic growth, trade, employment, political freedom or cultural values - from the perspective of people. It thus focuses on enlarging human choices - and it applies equally to developing and industrial counties.

Since 1990, when the first human development report was published by the UNDP, human development has been measured in terms of the Human Development Index (HDI). The HDI value is calculated every year for every country on the basis of life expectancy, adult literacy, mean years of schooling and per capita income. In addition to these basic factors, some other components are also taken into account to compute the index value for other aspects of human development. The final figures are then arranged in an order for comparison and to draw conclusions.

What is the Islamic approach to human development? The Arabic word *Islam* simply means 'submission', and is derived from a word *Salam* meaning peace. According to Muslim belief, 'Islam is a complete code of life'. This is because there is no aspect of life, such as religion, economy, politics, education, health etc., for which Islam does not provide guidance. The Qur'an and the Sunnah are the primary sources of knowledge for Muslims. One of the basic and the most important characteristics regarding the social economy and the economic system upon which the Qur'an repeatedly lays stress is that all means and resources through which human beings earn their livelihood are Divinely created.

In the Islamic way, human development is a purposeful activity aiming at: i) economic development with its fair distribution of benefits, ii) fair distribution should bring positive change in society; and, iii) both these activities should increase spiritual development. Interestingly, this approach is similar to – as well as different from

– the UNDP's concept of human development. It is similar in the sense that its first two points cover the components of human development which are defined by the UNDP. However, it differs in its emphasis on spiritual development and satisfaction. In Islamic philosophy, a human being is composed of soul and body; the soul is rational and spiritual and the body represents the animal and physical dimensions. Therefore, development is required in both these aspects. With reference to the above mentioned first two points regarding human development, Islam particularly emphasises: i) social justice, ii) universal aspiration to and access to knowledge and education, iii) economic development iv) maximum freedom of access to economic activity, and, v) improving the overall quality of life.

In this context, in Islam a preliminary step for human development is social security and the elimination of destitution. This approach differs from several other contemporary approaches such as the 'basic need approach' which is supported by the World Bank. This is due to the reason that in the former the anti-poverty programme is linked with social security while in the latter the main emphasis is on the fulfilment of the basic needs of human beings. In Islamic philosophy the social security component is a direct derivation from Qur'anic teachings where enormous emphasis is laid on social justice. With reference to this Islamic philosophy, a brief review of Islamic history regarding human development is presented in the following paragraphs.

In Islamic teachings there is much emphasis on human development and early Islamic history demonstrates its practicability. The first Muslim community was created on the global map in 622 CE, when the Messenger of Allah Muhammad ﷺ migrated from Makkah to Madinah. His ten-year rule over Madinah was a period of stability and development.

In this newly created community which was regulated mainly by the revelation and its tacit confirmation of some existing practice, Muslim and non-Muslim enjoyed their respective rights as stated in the clear contract made between them. It is appropriate to mention here that the innovative style of public administration as extrapolated in later ages was organised at four levels: i) Naqabat, ii) Arafat, iii) Nazarat, and, iv) Amalat.

Naqabat, which was the lowest administrative unit of the community, consisted of eight families among whom one of the heads of the families was its administrator. Arafat consisted of twelve Naqabats and was similar to a present day borough council. The head of an Arafat was called Areef and he was from the local people and approved by the government. In addition to administrative matters, he was responsible for the local treasury (*bait al-mal*). Nazarat was an intermediary administrative unit between Arafat and Amalat. Its function was similar to a county council. Each Nazarat consisted of twenty-four Arafats. Several Nazarats constituted an Amalat which was similar to a provincial government. The size of an Amalat depended upon the local socioeconomic situation and regional population. The chief executive of an Amalat was called Amil and he was directly appointed by the central government. Although the Amil was not the elected head of the region, the appointment was made after consultation with the people and social heads.

In the first community, the Prophet was its head. He ran community matters by regular consultation with his people. It was important that in matters governed by revelation his word was treated as final but in day-to-day matters, he sought the views of knowledgeable people. In fact, he created and developed this in such a way that governance was neither purely based on election nor on selection. He adopted a middle way in which there was more emphasis on the quality of advice rather than its quantity. This was compatible with the needs and nature of the people and therefore, during his short period of government, it was established on a sound footing and remained basically unchanged for centuries. Even during the middle period of Islamic history when the Islamic community stretched over three continents, this system worked efficiently.

It should be emphasised here that with reference to his teachings and political administration, the Prophet's ﷺ approach to human development was far in advance of any subsequent definition of human development. He placed enormous emphasis on education and the first message which he received from Allah was '*Iqra*', i.e., to read and learn.

During the period of the four right caliphs, the large Islamic community was divided into eight provinces and many new offices were established. One of the most important departments was the judiciary, i.e., the post of the 'Qadi' originally a function of the Caliph, which flourished very quickly. Another department was *Ifta'*, i.e., the issuing of fatwas, again originally a function of the Caliph and the knowledgeable people, and which had functions in common with the 'citizens' advice bureau' of developed countries. The equivalent of the Chancellor of Exchequer was the person responsible for the *Bait al-Mal*, who was required to be kind and benevolent to the public. While collecting *jizyah* from non-Muslims, the officials of this department had always to keep in mind the production and productivity of land, number of working people per household and genuine expenditures of the family. It was important that there was no injustice towards Muslims or non-Muslims and often Muslims were paying more in zakat as compared to non-Muslims' payment of *jizyah*.

In community development projects, *Nizart an-Nafi'ah* (almost like a department of civil engineering) played a leading role. This department was engaged in the construction of bridges, roads, police posts, public lodges, hostels and new cities. It has already been stated that during the time of the Caliph 'Umar, may Allah be pleased with him, this department prepared a feasibility study and maps to connect the Mediterranean to the Red Sea by a canal. Their plan and objective was similar to the present Suez Canal. The report was presented to the Caliph but after detailed consideration and discussion the project was not approved for security reasons. Although the Suez Canal was not built at that time, the lack of it was supplanted by constructing numerous other canals. In fact, there was a huge department for this purpose employing an army of workers.

The middle period of Islamic history is particularly famous because of its prosperity and advances in science and technology. This development was only possible due to the innovative steps and solid foundations laid by their predecessors. Like other Muslim rulers, the Caliph Mamun was very fond of academic activities and scientific research. He founded his House of Wisdom (*Bait al-Hikmah*), which housed a library as famous as any in medieval history and was a training centre for scholars. The same is also true for the 'Abode of Wisdom' (*Dar al-Hikmah*) in Cairo, which played an important role in the development of education. It would not be wrong to say that with respect to that age, Muslims were at the post-development stage and in this process their agriculture played a key role as a major source of employment which made possible a higher standard of health and longer life. This was the result of the efforts of government and Muslim scientists in establishing many agricultural research stations in Persia, Baghdad, Cairo and Cordoba. They grew new varieties of plants and used them in pharmacy. There were numerous community- or *awqaf*-run hospitals and clinics in the country which were closely coordination with these medicinal farms. In addition, they also established huge hospitals in major cities such as Damascus (in 707 CE), Cairo (874 CE) and Baghdad (918 CE). This is the reason that many western historians such as William Draper, S.P. Scott and Philip Hitti, clearly praise the human development of these middle period Muslims.

The above discussion reflects one of the main reasons of the success of past Muslims. Unfortunately, this success could not be maintained forever. What were the reasons for the decline of the Muslims? For some time the accepted notion among modern historians was that as a community or civilisation achieves ascendancy in a particular age, it inevitably results in its decline and fall. This theory seems valid *prima-facie* for the decline of Muslim power. However, one learns from history also that the Muslims laid the foundations of the Renaissance which throws into doubt the idea that the selfsame Muslims were at that time in decline.

A French historian discusses the progress of Islamic civilisation and how it motivated and empowered the general public. In his view it is childish to blame Islam for the decline of Muslims. Every nation has its period of glory. After a spell of splendour and glory a nation falls prey to negligence and slumber. A German historian Kramer attributes the decline to internecine feuds among Muslims. The Muslim Caliphate and sultanates disintegrated into small states whose rulers were given to mutual fighting. By the end of the eleventh century, this was the condition of the Muslim world when they faced the Crusaders. After a century when Muslims suffered Genghis Khan's invasion and found themselves vulnerable, they gathered all their resources and awoke from their slumber. According to Kramer, Muslims demolished their enemy not by the sword but with the help of their faith. The faith of Islam has such strength and resilience as enables its followers to take on any enemy, however powerful it may be. It inspired Muslims to emerge as victorious in all circumstances.

Muslims faced disintegration owing to unbalanced views that ran counter to the true spirit of Islam and on account of their preoccupation with peripheral issues. They were divided into many sects. As a result of preoccupation with worldly affairs and the influence of other civilisations they became indifferent to the message and teachings of Islam. Some took to opposing new knowledge. It led to the death of the creative spirit. Some promoted such ideas as gave rise to inaction and lassitude. Others went astray while some others took to the path of extremism. This political and religious inaction dealt a fatal blow to the institution of the Caliphate. Muslim rulers were given to un-Islamic ways of life, full of luxury, wantonness and extravagance, and in this the people imitated them and aspired to be like them.

While disregarding Qur'anic teachings, these rulers imposed exorbitant and illegal taxes on the public. When this burden became intolerable, 12,000 members of Banu Habib tribe, some three hundred years after the Prophet's ﷺ demise, opted for Christianity and migrated to the Roman empire. Little wonder then that Muslims gradually lost their power and glory and were relegated to the abyss of decline. Had Muslims been faithful in observing divine commands, they would not have fallen. The Prophet ﷺ is on record as indicating that knowledge is superior to ignorant worship. Had Muslims not neglected Qur'anic commands, they would not have ended up as a backward community.

6.2 State of the Contemporary Muslim World

It is noteworthy that for nearly thirteen centuries, i.e., from 632 to 1924 CE, Islam spread over the world and the *Ummah* remained intact. Nevertheless, rivalries for power within the Caliphate eroded its effectiveness, and the *Ummah* as a designation of the political unity of the Muslim world gradually dissolved. As the Caliphate crumbled, its political authority disintegrated in the hands of those who paid every price to wield it and the vacuum was filled increasingly by foreign powers. In fact, until the first quarter of the twentieth century, the Muslims remained more or less united under the umbrella of the Caliphate. After the collapse of this institution, the vast Muslim *Dawlah* disintegrated into many parts and various independent states emerged on the global map. Thus the contemporary shape of present Muslim world is totally different than it was under Caliphate. While drawing the contemporary picture of the Muslim world, Abu Sulayman says in his book (entitled: *Towards an Islamic Theory of International Relations*):

> Internally weak, relatively backward, frustrated, conflict-ridden, suffering from internal tensions, and often controlled and abused by foreign powers, the Muslim world is in a state of crisis. For Muslims, all modern history is a tragedy. At an earlier time, during the sweeping revolution of Islam, Muslims were the custodians of civilisation and both the centre and masters of the civilisation. But at present, the Muslim polity is neither master nor partner, and both Muslims and Islam are often regarded in world

politics as little more than problematic. How did such a state of affairs come about, and in what ways can the Muslim peoples alter this condition?

In Muslim countries it is customary to blame external powers and imperialism for all manners of ills. Although this habit may point up many of the grievances and obstacles Muslims face, it cannot explain the internal cause of the ills. These ills put in motion a process of decay that dissipated the internal powers of the Muslim world. The resultant weakness brought external powers into the picture, complicating the difficulties. The problem of the external factors, along with the complications they caused for the Muslim world, cannot be dealt with before the internal factors are fully understood.

It reflects the fact that the Muslim world is today perched on the horns of an excruciating dilemma. It has been subjected to colonial domination for a very long time and has only recently extricated itself from the West's stranglehold. Although its struggle against colonialism has achieved major successes, it has yet to go a long way in breaking the intellectual, psychological, cultural, economic and technological chains. The crisis that engulfed the Muslim world during the last three centuries, can be attributed both to external and internal factors.

Presently, the problem is that, in addition to accusing others, Muslim scholars have been misleading themselves with their reading of Islam's magnificent past and imagination of a utopian future without confronting the realities of the modern world where thoughtful and rational considerations have little room for sentimental responses. The current Muslim states have also not been able to present themselves as role models. However, Islam cannot be held responsible for it. Islamists often misinterpret Islam as they ignore the vital issues of poverty, hunger, inadequacy and widespread illiteracy that limit social justice and societal transformation. This is one of the main reasons why in many

Muslim countries, social problems are so deeply rooted - they left the community very vulnerable. The ultimate impact of such social weaknesses is not only internal, but it also adversely affects the overall global position of Muslims.

It is worth mentioning here that Muslims constitute nearly a quarter of the global population. According to recent estimates, out of a global population of 5.87 billion, 1.31 billion (22.2%) were Muslims at the time of the study. Similarly, of the total 103 million km^2 of geographic area of the world, Muslims occupy 30.5 million km^2 (22.8%). The global map indicates that the Muslim world stretches from North West Africa (Morocco) to South East Asia (Indonesia). It ranges form the Atlantic to the Pacific, the Mediterranean Sea and Indian Ocean, and controls the gateways of the world's trade and commerce, such as the straits of Gibraltar, Bosphorus, Hormuz, Malaka and the Suez Canal. It is further estimated that Muslim countries produce more than two-thirds of the world's oil, 70 percent of its rubber, 75 percent of the jute, 67 percent of the spices, two-thirds of the palm oil, and half of all tin and phosphates. In addition, they have a vast number of gas reserves, and also produce a large quantity of the world's cotton, tea, coffee, wool, uranium, manganese, cobalt and many other commodities and minerals.

However, in spite of the above advantages, the Muslim world is far behind the non-Muslim world in terms of economic development. In its *World Development Reports 1999-2000*, the World Bank reveals that around 26 percent of people in the developing and the transitional economies' countries were living below the poverty line. The analysis with regard to the Muslim countries indicates that nearly one-third of the population of the low-income Muslim countries are living below the poverty line. This is one of the main reasons that the Muslim world faces a number of challenges. The situation of individual Muslim countries also presents a bleak picture. Some countries are either facing the problem of civil war or warlike situations. In addition, according to available statistics, Gambia, Mauritania, Uganda, Kazakhstan,

Kyrgyzstan, Turkmenistan and Uzbekistan are among the poorest countries in the world in which the majority of the population lives below the poverty line. There are some other countries, e.g., Burkina Faso, Chad, Guinea Bissau and Tunisia, where per capita GDP is less than US$ 250. Widespread illiteracy is another major evil in the Muslim world. Sadly, Niger with its 14 percent literacy rate is the most illiterate country in the world, followed by Burkina Faso (21%) and Gambia (33%). It is common knowledge that poverty, illiteracy and internal instability also have affects on the state of health of a country. Thus, the lowest life expectancy in the world can also be seen in Muslim countries: Afghanistan and Burkina Faso; in which life-expectancy is only 45 years.

This situation also presents the overall picture of human development of the Muslim world. Furthermore, human development rankings of Muslim countries are generally lower than per capita income rankings, showing that even their relatively tiny incomes have not been fully pop popd into the lives of their people. The overall 'human development index' for fifty-two Muslim countries is much lower than the overall 'human development index' of non-Muslim countries. The value of the 'human development index' can be judged from the fact that it is an aggregate value of life expectancy, adult literacy, mean years of schooling and per capita income. According to the United Nations *Human Development Report 1999,* as many as forty-five Muslim countries had a lower value on the 'human development index' compared to the world's average. This alarming situation underlines the fact that some drastic measures are needed for improvement.

6.3 The Ummah and the 21st Century

The current situation of globalisation and the state of underdevelopment of the Muslim world demand urgent measures for improvement. Unless the ruling élites of the Muslim countries realise how severe are the problems, and make a political commitment, the situation in future could be far, far worse. The current situation of the Muslim world demands comprehensive planning for the future of the Muslim Ummah. The discussion in the following paragraphs suggests that short, medium and long term strategies should be adopted for this purpose. These three periods can be segmented as: period one; 2005-2015, period two; 2016-2030 and period three; 2031-2050. The time from now to 2005 should be utilised for mutual consultation to develop a consensus and political commitment among Muslim countries. This whole process would need to establish some new initiatives as well as strengthening various existing institutions of the Muslim world.

One of the most important points with regard to the success of the Muslim world is the establishment of the Organisation of Islamic Countries (OIC) itself. There is no other example in the world where such a large number of countries have joined together only on the basis of religion. No matter how weak this Organisation is - at least it could provide a base for all activities of future development of the Muslim world. Thus the steps discussed in the following paragraphs should be based on the platform of the OIC, as the Muslim world has no other alternative. In the contemporary global environment, it is noteworthy that initially any future economic cooperation among Muslim countries cannot be successful unless there is a valid economic motive behind it. In the context of the above stated approach to development; in 'period one' - 2005-2015 (i.e., the short-term strategy), Muslim countries have to make efforts on at least five important fronts:

- A sound unified financial system for the Muslim World
- A common Islamic market for the promotion of mutual trade
- Advances in the fields of science and technology, particularly in low-cost technologies which do not require massive capitalisation
- Well established media and news agencies
- Establishment of an Islamic Security Council and an Islamic Defence Force.

It is beyond the reach of this brief discussion to present a detailed analytical case study for each component. There is a lot of potential for international trade between Muslim countries and research has already been conducted on various aspects of economic cooperation. Here, the objective is only to present a framework for this approach. Under the circumstances, first of all, Muslim countries should take initiatives in the promotion of mutual trade. Now is the time for Muslim countries to realise that they must not be used as a dumping ground for second-rate goods and services from Western industrial countries; they have to develop their own market. Initially, they should focus on regional and sub-regional economic unions, e.g., Arab Common Market, Arab Maghrib Union, the Gulf Cooperation Council and Economic Cooperation Organisation, etc. When this cooperation is strengthened, then the next step should be cooperation between the regional economic groups leading to the development of a full-fledged Islamic common market. This task is not difficult to achieve; due to the compact geographical position of the Muslim countries, they have a comparative advantage in trading with each other over trading with Western industrial countries. It is particularly true in the case of the cost of transportation, which will be far lower in intra-*Ummah* trade as compared to trade with Australia, American or the European Union. Moreover, as they all are developing countries, their costs of production are also much lower than those of the Western world, which means that due to economies of scale they have an additional advantage in mutual trade.

It is common knowledge that the Muslim world is weighed down under the huge burden of foreign debt, particularly that owed to the IMF and the World Bank. At present the situation is that both these global moneylending institutions are receiving huge amounts of interest on loans which they have advanced to many countries. The amount received as interest is utilised to advance further loans to countries to pay back their interest or just to keep them going. There are some countries that have repaid more than the amount of the loan that they received from these institutions. Under the current global circumstances there is no way out of this vicious circle. This alarming situation demands action from the ruling authorities of the Muslim countries to develop a positive strategy. It is therefore, necessary to create and strengthen Islamic financial initiatives.

The ruling families of several Muslim countries have large amounts of financial reserves in Western banks and investments in their stock exchanges. It is essential that a significant part of this money should be invested in Islamic financial initiatives. Furthermore, a Muslim Monetary Fund (MMF) should be established whose primary objective should be to take Muslim countries out of the vicious circle of foreign debts. This action would drastically reduce the financial burden on the annual budgets of these countries, thus more resources would be available to tackle the problems of poverty and underdevelopment. It would also enable them to initiate various projects that would generate income and employment opportunities. In addition to the MMF, the Muslim World also needs to establish a Human Development Fund (HDF). At the initial stage this money should be utilised to establish a network of basic infrastructure and start various human development projects in deprived communities in the Muslim countries. In all of this, they would draw attention to the futuristic nature of the commercial shari'ah of Islam and its very real potential to realise a genuinely benign, post-capitalist mode of economic transaction. In particular, we note the efforts to restore gold and silver as Islamic currencies – an effort supported by no less a statesman than Mohammad Mahathir the prime minister of Malaysia and supported theoretically by many non-Muslim economists such as Alan Greenspan – as well as the efforts to restore the whole complex of Islamic trading modes such as 'profit and loss' sharing transactions, and *awqaf* endowments, etc.

It does not need to be emphasised that the Muslim world is lagging behind in the field of science and technology. The same is also true of media. In both fields the Muslim world is totally dependent upon the West. Due to this weakness of the Muslim world, major global players are taking full advantage of this situation. This is one of the main reasons that the Muslim countries have no voice and weight in global affairs. The current global situation demands that Muslim countries should have their own satellites. Some Muslim countries have gained the technological skills but are unable to launch a programme due to financial constraints. However, this hurdle can be removed by initiating joint-ventures with rich Muslim countries that do not possess such skills. These initiatives will provide a sound base for development of Muslim media and information technology, which are the key elements for playing a leading role in global affairs. These efforts will not only help to project the Islamic cause in the world but will also help the Western world to better understand the Muslim world. It may be expedient that as a first step, regions should develop their own media policies, followed by a more comprehensive and integrated policy of the Muslim world as a whole. This would require a team of experts creating the desired impact and maintaining an overall harmony and balance in the projection of themes and ideas. Muslim media must embark upon a campaign of truth, particularly to impress upon the world that the cause of peace in the world is achievable through cooperation and communication.

In this age, the concept of security has become broader and refined in shape. Thus in addition to the military power of a country, it also encompasses local, regional, political and economic issues. One of the most important issues is that despite widespread poverty, illiteracy, hunger and debt burden, Muslim countries are forced to allocate a chunk of their financial resources to the defence sector, which is mainly due to internal and external threats to their security. It is estimated that during 2000 they spent around US$85 billion on defence and that nearly six million people were engaged in this sector. It is important that with mutual cooperation of the Muslim countries, a large amount of financial and human resources could be saved and utilised in other productive sectors.

Several Muslim countries have been and are, facing many problems of internal instability, conflict and war. The Palestine crises, Iran-Iraq war, Gulf War, Afghanistan, Kashmir, Sudan,

Western Sahara, Indonesia and East Timor are clear to see. In all these crises, the role of the major global players, UNO and OIC need not be explained. There is an urgent need that Muslim countries should create their own Islamic Security Council (ISC). This council should have two objectives. First, on the political front, it should be the supreme authority for dealing with internal and external conflicts in the Muslim world. Second, it should be the governing authority of a strong joint Islamic Defence Force (IDF) to respond to any aggression by a member state. The question is how to establish this force? Muslim countries should consider saving on defence expenditures and human resources. It would be in their mutual interest that if from 2005, as a first step, they make a cut of one percent in their defence budgets which should be increased to 10 percent by 2015. This reduction would save more than US$45 billion. Some of this money could be utilised to expand the activities of Islamic financial initiatives while the rest could be used to establish an Islamic Defence Force. The overall strength of the IDF should be not less than one million personnel. More or less like NATO, an IDF could play an effective role in preventing internal or external threats to the Muslim world. The advantages of the establishment of an IDF would be multifarious and not limited to security issues. It would give confidence to Muslim countries to solve their own problems independently rather than depending upon major global players. With the passage of time, an IDF would be useful in tackling the unjust monopolies of Western countries and thus would keep the balance of power in global affairs. It is hoped that in the presence of an IDF, problems such as the Iran-Iraq war, the Gulf War, the occupation of Palestine and al-Quds would not happen in the future.

Another point of primary importance is that due to the imbalance of power within the UN Security Council, the five permanent members enjoy an undue and unjust monopoly. Recently, some other countries have been very active in attempting to secure a permanent seat in the UN Security Council. Muslim countries must also try to secure at least one permanent seat on this Council. This seat should be cooperatively managed through the OIC. It is important that with regard to this whole proposed programme, the above mentioned activities have to be completed in 'period-one' (2005-2015 CE). When this has been established on sound ground, further measures are needed in 'period-two' (2016-2030). In this period, steps should be taken to merge the economies and political activities of Muslim countries. By the end of this fifteen year period:

- There should be a single currency of all OIC member countries, preferably return to the use of gold and silver.
- The revival of the whole modus of Islamic financing through 'profit and loss' sharing transactions such as *qirad* and *mudarabah*, and the recreation of guilds in the zone of manufacture and the restoration of their functioning as sources of financial capital for members, as well as the recreation of the nexus of *awqaf*-endowments.
- An IDF should have been established as a single joint defence force for the whole Muslim world.
- The debt burden and poverty have to be eliminated to a great extent.
- In strengthening the OIC, the status, role and authority of the head of this institution should be more than a formal Secretary General.
- By the completion of these objectives, this transitional period should lead to a foundation for the overall strengthening of the integration of Islamic countries.

After the completion of the above steps, the third and the final phase (2031-2050 CE) should complete the process of unification, ending with the establishment of the 'United States of Islam' (USI). The strategy of unification should be adopted in such a way that at apex level there should be a loose federation of member states. By keeping sufficient internal autonomy, all Muslim countries should be autonomous in their internal affairs while the four major sectors, i.e., currency, defence, foreign affairs and communication should be under the control of a 'federal-body'. This would provide enormous politico-economic benefits to the masses of the Muslim world. By the end of this stage (2050 CE), the OIC should be converted into a 'federal governing body' of the Muslim world and the position of the then Secretary General should be changed to a formal Caliph. This federation of Muslim countries should be based on principles of mutual consultation as were the first community in Madinah and the best periods of Islamic governance. Much exercise and research is needed to make this framework compatible with the requirements of the modern age.

In the contemporary global environment and due to the declining state of the Muslim world, the above proposal does not seem much more than a dream. However, if it is a dream, it is the dream of the masses of the Muslims spread from East Asia to West Africa, and history suggests that dreams have the potential to become reality. Two centuries ago, who thought that more than four dozen North American states would be united into one country and it would be the only superpower of the world? A century ago, did anyone imagine that the European states, which have completely separate cultures, languages, state systems as well as a long history of mutual war culminating in two 'world wars', would be a progressive union? More recently, only two decades ago, who would have thought that the Soviet Union, a nuclear superpower would be defeated by an extremely poor country like Afghanistan and later, disintegrate into several parts due to bankruptcy?

When considering the process of the formation of a 'union' by the North American and European states, Muslim countries have an added advantage: they have a common culture, history, beliefs and above all a widespread desire for this integration at grassroots level. Deriving strength from its rich tradition, the Muslim community has the potential to set an example for the rest of the world. Thus there is the need to develop appropriate strategies to realise this dream. The ruling classes of the Muslim countries must realise that, rather than begging from others, this is the only way for development – not only for the Muslim masses but also for the elite.

A careful consideration of this approach indicates that not only is it essential for unity among Muslim countries - it is also important to promote an effective role for the Muslim world in global affairs. Thus it is composed of two components: internal and external. The internal component is unity within the Muslim world while the external component is its relations with the outside world. The contemporary global situation demands a rational interpretation of Islam along with the mobilisation of the political power of the Muslim world. There is a need to highlight the fact that Islam does not prohibit Muslims working with the Western world on matters of common interest. Thus efforts should be made to promote mutual trust between the Muslim and the non-Muslim worlds. Muslim countries must try to avoid confrontation with the West. They must evolve and reshape policies in a manner that, instead of animosity, promotes a spirit of mutual understanding and good will. This is a very challenging task but they have to accomplish it, as it is a question of their survival in the future. Therefore, they must strive for better relationships. The areas of convergence need to be emphasised and carefully worked upon, whereas the areas of divergence need to be seriously looked into, in order to defuse tension. It is beyond doubt that these activities will not only be in the interest of the Muslim world, they would be helpful in the promotion of global stability, peace and prosperity.

It is important in the accomplishment of this whole package, that two simultaneous approaches in the internal and external sectors are adopted. Regarding the internal sector, the most important step is that in collaboration with the general public, liberal and moderate Muslim intellectuals and politicians should jointly establish pressure groups and by gaining public opinion within the country, various evolutionary movements have to be developed to eliminate social evils. At the level of the *Ummah*, such national movements should have close coordination amongst themselves to influence the governments of Muslim countries. They need to put moral and political pressure on their own respective governments to promote coordination among the

Muslim countries. The objective of this approach ought not to be to bring about a revolution within the Muslim world, which might lead to a disaster, rather that it should start a peaceful and social evolutionary process at grassroots level. Such efforts in various Muslim countries would be helpful in creating internal solidarity and stability, and external coordination and harmony at the level of the *Ummah*. This process would initiate a new era of development, insha'Allah.

Further Reading

Abdul-Haleem, Harfiah, *Islam and the Environment*, London: Ta-Ha Publishers, 1998.

Abdul-Mabud, Shaikh, *Theory of Evolution: An Assessment from The Islamic Point of View*, Cambridge: The Islamic Academy, 1991.

AbuSulayman, AbdulHamid A., *Towards the Islamic Theory of International Relations: New Directions for Methodology and Thought*, Herndon: The International Institute of Islamic Thought, 1994.

Adahl, Karin and Mikael Ahlund, *Islamic Art Collections*, London: Curzon Press, 1999.

Ahsan, Abdullah al, *OIC: The Organisation of the Islamic Conference*, Herndon: The International Institute of Islamic Thought, 1988.

Ahsan, Muhammad and Muhammad Munir, *Science and Art in Medieval Islam* (Urdu), Rawalpindi: Foundation for Research on International Environment National Development and Security, 2000.

Ahsan, Muhammad, 'Globalisation and the Muslim World: A Case Study of Pakistan', in Ali Mohammadi (ed.), *Islam Encountering Globalisation*, London: Curzon Press, 2002 (fourth coming).

Ahsan, Muhammad, 'Human Development Strategies and the Muslim World: A Multidimensional Approach', *National Development and Security*, Vol. 3-3, February 1999.

Ahsan, Muhammad, 'Population Administration during the Time of First Four Caliphs (RA)' (Urdu), *Ham Loug*, Vol. 7, January-June 1992.

Ahsan, Muhammad, 'Population Administration during the Time of Prophet Mohammad ﷺ' (Urdu), *Ham Loug*, Vol. 6, July-December 1991.

Ahsan, Muhammad, 'Population Administration of Medieval Muslims' (Urdu), *Ham Loug*, Vol. 8, July-December 1992.

Ahsan, Muhammad, 'The Twenty-first Century and the Muslim World: State of Human Development with particular Reference to Education', *Muslim Education Quarterly*, Vol. 16-3, 1999.

Ahsan, Muhammad, *Environment, Human Security and Islam: A Case Study of Pakistan*, a paper presented in 'Seminar on the Environment, Education and Religion', organised by the University of Cambridge and The Islamic Academy, Cambridge, March 2001.

Ahsan, Muhammad, Fatima Munir, *Muslim Agriculture in Medieval Age* (Urdu), Rawalpindi: Foundation for Research on International Environment National Development and Security, 2000.

Ahsan, Muhammad, *Pan-Islamism? Peace and Prosperity in the Twenty-first Century*, a paper presented in 'International Conference on Cosmopolis: Democratisation Global Economy and Culture', organised by University of Helsinki, June 2000.

Al-Andalusi, Sa'id, *Science in Medieval World: Book of the Categories of Nations*, (translated and edited by Sema'an I. Salem and Alok Kumar), Austin: University of Texas Press, 1991.

Al-Hassan, Ahmad and Donald R. Hill, *Islamic Technology: An Illustrated History*, Cambridge: Cambridge University Press, 1986.

Anawati, G., 'Science', in P.M. Holt, et. al., *Cambridge History of Islam* (Vol. II), Cambridge: Cambridge University Press, 1970.

Ardalan, N. and L. Bakhtair, *The Sense of Unity: The Sufi Tradition in Persian Architecture*, Chicago: Chicago University Press, 1973.

Arkoun, Mohammed, *Islam, Europe and the West*, London: I.B. Tauris, 1996.

Atil, Esin, *Art of the Arab World*, Washington: Smithsonian Institutions, 1975.

Bakar, Osman, *Classification of Knowledge in Islam: A Study in Islamic Philosophies of Science*, Cambridge: The Islamic Text Society, 1998.

Baker, Osman, *The History and Philosophy of Islamic Science*, Cambridge: The Islamic Text Society, 2000.

Blair, Sheila S. and Bloom, Jonathan M., *The Art and Architecture of Islam*, New Haven: Yale University Press, 1994.

Brend, Barbara, *Islamic Art*, London: British Museum Press, 1991.

Brown, Edward G., *Arabian Medicine*, Cambridge: Cambridge University Press, 1961.

Bucaille, Maurice, *The Bible, the Qur'an and Science*, Indianapolis: American Trust Publications, 1978.

Castello-Cortes, Ian, *et. al.* (eds.), *World Reference Atlas*, London: Dorling Kindersley Ltd., 1999.

Clagett, M. *The Science of Mechanics in the Middle Ages*, Madison: Michigan State University Press, 1951.

Cook, M.A., *Studies in the Economic History of the Middle East from the Rise of Islam to the Present Day*, London: Curzon Press, 1970.

Djait, Hichem, *Europe and Islam* (trans.: Peter Heinegg), Berkley: University of California Press, 1985.

Elgood, C., *A Medical History of Persia and the Eastern Caliphate*, Cambridge: Cambridge University Press, 1951.

Eliade, Mircea, *The Forge and the Crucible: the Origin and Structure of Alchemy* (trans.: Stephen Corrin), Chicago: University of Chicago Press, 1978.

Espesito, John L. (ed.), *The Oxford Encyclopaedia of the Modern Islamic World*: New York: Oxford University Press, 1995.

Esposito, John L. *Islam in Asia*, New York: Oxford University Press, 1987.

Esposito, John L., *The Oxford History of Islam*, New York: Oxford University Press, 2000.

Ettinghausen, Richard and Oleg Grabar, *The Art and Architecture of Islam 650-1250*, New Haven: Yale University Press, 1992.

Fletcher, Richard, *Moorish Spain*, London, Weidenfield and Nicholson, 1992.

Geertz, Clifford, *Islam Observed: Religious Development in Morocco and Indonesia*, Chicago: Chicago University Press, 1971.

Gillispie, C.C. (ed.), *Dictionary of Scientific Biography*, New York: Scriber, 1980.

Glasse, Cyril, *Concise Encyclopaedia of Islam*, San Francisco: Harper and Row, 1980.

Goldstein, Thomas, *Dawn of Modern Science: From Arabs to Leonardo de Vinci*, Boston: Houghton Mifflin, 1980.

Grabar, Oleg, *The Foundation of Islamic Art*, New Haven: Yale University Press, 1988.

Grube, Ernst, et. al., *Islamic Art*, London: Oxford University Press, 1999.

Grunebeaum, Gustav (ed.), 'Muslim World View and Muslim Science', in *Islam: Essays in the Nature and Growth of a Cultural Tradition*, Menasha: American Anthropological Association, 1954.

Hamarneh, Sami K., *Health Science in Early Islam* (edited by Munawar A. Anees), San Antonio: Noor Health Foundation, 1985.

Hayes, John R. (ed.), *The Genius of Arab Civilization*, Cambridge: MIT Press, 1983.

Hill, Donald R., *Islamic Science and Engineering*, Edinburgh: Edinburgh University Press, 1994.

Hiskett, Mervyn, *The Course of Islam in Africa*, Edinburgh: Edinburgh University Press, 1994.

Hitti, Philip K., *History of the Arabs from the Earliest Times to the Present*, London: Macmillan, 1968.

Holt, Peter Malcolm, et. al., *The Cambridge History of Islam*, Cambridge: Cambridge University Press, 1978.

Hoodbhoy, Pervez, *Islam and Science: Religious Orthodoxy and the*

Battle for Rationality, London: Zed Books, 1991.

Hourani, Albert, *A History of the Arab Peoples*, Cambridge, M.A.: Harvard University Press, 1992.

King, David A., *Astronomy in the Service of Islam*, Aldershot: Variorum, 1993.

King, David A., *Catalogue of Scientific Manuscript in the Egyptian National Library*, Cairo: Egyptian Book Organisation, 1985.

Landau, Rom, *Arab Contribution to Civilization*, San Francisco: American Academy of Asian Studies, 1958.

Lewis, Bernard, et. al., *Islam and the Arab World: Faith, People and Culture*, New York: American Heritage Publishing Co., 1976.

Lewis, Bernard, *The Middle East: A Brief History of the Last 2000 Years*, New York: Scribner, 1996.

Lewis, Bernard, *The Muslim Discovery of Europe*, New York: W.W. Norton, 1982.

Lindberg, David, *The Beginning of Western Science: The European Scientific Tradition in Philosophical, Religious and Institutional Context, 600 BC to AD 1450*, Chicago: University of Chicago Press, 1992.

Ludden, David, *An Agrarian History of South Asia*, Cambridge: Cambridge University Press, 1999.

Lunde, Paul, et. al., 'Science: The Islamic Legacy', *Aramco World*, Vol. 33-33, May-June 1982, New York: Aramco Corporation, 1982.

Mansfield, Peter, *A History of the Middle East*, London: Penguin Books, 1992.

Mason, Stephen F., *A History of the Science*, New York: Collier Books, 1962.

Munson, Henry, *Islam and Revolution in the Middle East*, New Haven: Yale University Press, 1989.

Murdoch, John E., *Album of Science: Antiquity and Middle Ages*, New York: Scribner, 1984.

Nasr, Seyyed Hossein, *An Introduction to Islamic Cosmological Doctrines*, Boulder: Shambhala, 1978.

Nasr, Seyyed Hossein, *Islamic Art: An Illustrated Study*, London: World of Islam Festival Publishing Co., Ltd., 1976.

Nasr, Seyyed Hossein, *Islamic Science: An Illustrated Study*, London: World of Islam Festival Publishing Co., Ltd., 1976.

Nasr, Seyyed Hossein, *Religion and the Order of Nature*, New York: Oxford University Press, 1996.

Nasr, Seyyed Hossein, *Science and Civilisation in Islam*, Cambridge: The Islamic Text Society, 1987.

Nasr, Seyyed Hossein, *The Need for a Sacred Science*, London: Curzon Press, 1993.

New Internationalist Publications Ltd., *The World Guide*, Oxford: New Internationalist Publications Ltd., 2000.

Nicholson, Reynold, *A Literary History of the Arabs*, London: Curzon Press, 1995.

Price, Derek D., *Science since Babylon*, New Haven: Yale University Press, 1975.

Qadir, C.A., *Philosophy and Science in the Islamic World*, London: Routledge, 1988.

Quick, Abdullah Hakim, *Deeper Roots*, London, Ta-Ha Publishing Ltd., 1996,

Ragep, F. Jamil (ed. & trans.), *Nasir al-Din al-Tusi's Memoir on Astronomy*, New York: Springer-Verlag, 1993.

Rashid, Roshdi, *et. al.* (eds.), *Encyclopaedia of the History of Arab Science*, London: Routledge, 1996.

Rehman, Fazul ur, *Islam*, Chicago: University of Chicago Press, 1979.

Robinson, Francis, *Islam and Muslim History in South Asia*, New Delhi: Oxford University Press, 2000.

Rodinson, Maxime, *Europe and the Mystique of Islam*, London, I.B. Tauris, 1988.

Rosenthal, Franz, *The Classical Heritage in Islam*, London: Routledge & Kegan Paul, 1975.

Sabra, A.I, 'The Scientific Enterprise', in *Islam and the Arab World*, New York: Alfred A, Knopf, 1979.

Saliba, George, *A History of Arabic Astronomy: Planetary Theories during the Golden Age of Islam*, New York: New York University Press, 1994.

Sardar, Ziauddin (ed.), *The Touch of Midas: Science, Values and Environment in Islam and the West*, Manchester: Manchester University Press, 1984.

Sarton, George, *A Guide to the History of Science*, New York: Ronald Press, 1952.

Sarton, George, *Introduction to the History of Science*, Melbourne, FL: Krieger Publishing Co, 1948.

Sarton, George, *The History of Science and the New Humanism*, Midland: Indiana University Press, 1931.

Sarwar, Ghulam (ed.), *OIC: Contemporary Issues and the Muslim World*, Rawalpindi: Foundation for Research on International Environment National Development and Security, 1997.

Sarwar, Ghulam, *Islam: Belief and Teachings*, London: The Muslim Educational Trust, 1994.

Sayili, Aydin, *The Observatory in Islam and its Place in the General History of the Observatory*, North Stratford: NH-Ayer Publishers, 1981.

Schacht, J. and C.H. Bosworth (eds.), *The Legacy of Islam*, Oxford: Clarendon Press, 1974.

Sims, Eleanor G., 'Printing in Timurid Iran', *Asian Art*, Vol. II-2, Spring 1989.

Singer, Charles Joseph, *A Short History of Scientific Ideas to 1900*, New York: Oxford University Press, 1959.

Smith, Savage, et. al., *Islamic Geomancy and a Thirteenth Century Divinatory Device*, Malibu: Undena Publications, 1980.

Stewart, Desmond, *Early Islam*, New York: Time Inc. 1967.

Thorndike, Lynn, *A History of Magic and Experimental Science*,

New York: Columbia University Press, 1958.

Trimingham, John Spencer, *The Influence of Islam Upon Africa*, London: Longman, 1980.

Turner, Howard R., *Science in Medieval Islam*, Austin: University of Texas Press, 1997.

Ullmann, Manfred, *Islamic Survey II: Islamic Medicine*, Edinburgh: Edinburgh University Press, 1978.

UNDP, *Human Development Report 2000*, New York: Oxford University Press, 2000.

UNESCO, *Islam, Philosophy and Science*, Paris: United Nations Scientific and Cultural Organisation, 1982.

Watt, W. Montgomery, *The Influence of Islam on Medieval Europe*, Edinburgh: Edinburgh University Press, 1972.

Wijdan Ali, *The Arab Contribution to Islamic Art*, Cairo: The American University in Cairo, 2000.

World Bank, *World Development Indicators 2000*, Washington, D.C.: The World Bank, 2000.

World Bank, *World Development Report 2000/2001*, New York: Oxford University Press, 2000.

Young, M., et. al. (eds.), *Religion, Learning and Science in the Abbasid Period*, Cambridge: Cambridge University Press, 1990.

Basic Data on the Muslim World

Country	Population Millions 1998	Surface Area 000 km²	GNP (US$) Total in billion	GNP (US$) Per capita	Population blow poverty line	GDP Growth Rate 1975-00
Afghanistan	26 (99)	652	2.7	164	..	..
Albania	3 (70)	29	2.7	810	19.6	-1.3
Algeria	30 (99)	2,382	46.5	1,550	22.6	0.1
Azerbaijan	8 (93)	87	3.9	490	..	-11.8
Bahrain	0.6 (100)	1	4.9	7,660	..	-1.4
Bangladesh	126 (87)	144	44.0	350	35.6	2.2
Benin	6 (15)	113	2.3	380	33.0	0.7
Brunei	0.3 (63)	6	9.0	30,000	..	-1.0
Burkina Faso	11 (25)	274	2.6	240	..	1.2
Cameroon	14 (16)	475	8.7	610	..	0.1
Chad	7 (45)	1,284	1.7	230	..	0.3
Comoros	0.5 (86)	2	0.2	370	..	-1.1
Djibouti	0.6 (94)	23	0.5	960	..	..
Egypt	61 (96)	1,001	79.2	1,290	..	3.6
Gabon	1 (..)	268	4.6	3,950	..	-1.6
Gambia	1 (96)	11	0.4	340	64.0	-0.1
Guinea	7 (85)	247	3.8	450	..	1.4
Guinea Bissau	1 (90)	36	0.2	160	49.0	0.3
Indonesia	204 (90)	1,905	138.5	680	15.1	5.1
Iran	62 (99)	1,633	109.6	1,770	..	-1.6
Iraq	22 (98)	438	20.0	1,036	..	-11.2

Jordan	5 (92)	89	6.9	1,520	15.0	2.3
Kazakhstan	16 (47)	2,717	20.6	1,310	65.0	-6.6
Kuwait	2 (85)	18	32.8	16,400	..	-1.5
Kyrgyzstan	5 (75)	199	1.6	350	88.0	9.4
Lebanon	4 (57)	10	15.0	3,560	..	..
Libya	5 (97)	1760	23.3	4,755	..	-4.5
Malaysia	22 (53)	330	79.8	3,600	16.0	4.6
Maldives	0.3 (100)	0.3	0.3	1,230	..	5.4
Mali	11 (90)	1,240	2.6	250	..	0.6
Mauritania	3 (100)	1,026	1.0	410	57.0	0.0
Morocco	28 (99)	447	34.8	1,250	..	1.7
Niger	10 (80)	1,267	1.9	190	13.1	-1.7
Nigeria	121 (70)	924	36.4	300	34.1	-0.5
Oman	2 (98)	213	10.3	6,440	..	2.1
Pakistan	132 (96)	796	63.2	480	34.0	2.9
Palestine	3 (75)	6	..	..	..	..
Qatar	0.7 (95)	11	7.0	14,000	..	..
Saudi Arabia	21 (100)	2,150	105.0	6.610	..	-2.6
Senegal	9 (92)	197	4.8	530	..	-0.3
Sierra Leone	5 (70)	72	0.7	140	75.0	-2.2
Somalia	10 (100)	638	0.8	80	..	..
Sudan	28 (75)	2,506	7.2	269	..	-0.9
Syria	15 (92)	185	15.6	1,020	..	1.2
Tajikistan	6 (95)	143	2.1	350	..	-11.2
Tunisia	9 (98)	164	19.2	210	14.1	2.5

Turkey	63 (99)	775	200.0	3,160	..	2.0
Turkmenistan	5 (85)	448	6.4	1,650	61.0	..
U.A.E	3 (96)	84	48.7	18,220	..	-2.9
Uganda	21 (25)	241	6.7	320	55.0	1.9
Uzbekistan	24 (88)	447	20.9	870	63.0	..
Yemen	16 (97)	528	4.9	300	..	..

Note: Figures of population in parenthesis are the percentage of Muslim population in the respective countries.

Chronology of Prophetic Events

Fazlur Rehman Shaikh

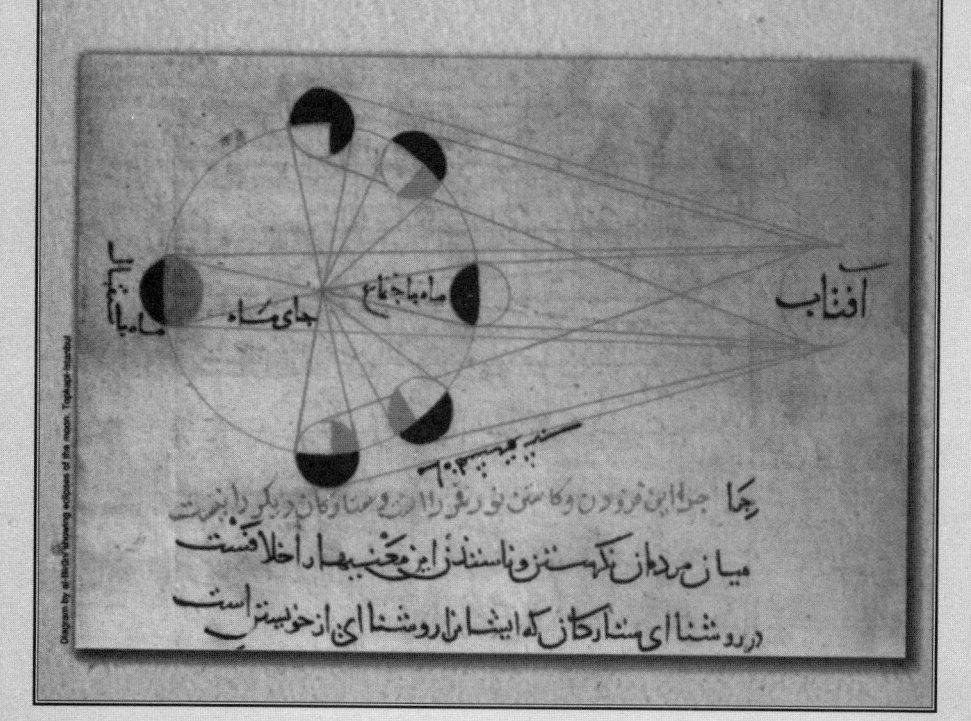